"Alas, Poor Ghost!"

Traditions of Belief in Story and Discourse

"Alas, Poor Ghost!"

Traditions of Belief
in
Story and Discourse

by
Gillian Bennett

New, Expanded, and Extensively Revised Edition of
Traditions of Belief: Women and the Supernatural

Utah State University Press
Logan, Utah

Utah State University Press
Logan, Utah 84322-7800

Typography by WolfPack

Text design by Chantze Kin

Cover Design by Barbara Yale-Read

Library of Congress Cataloging-in-Publication Data

Bennett, Gillian.
    Alas, poor ghost! : traditions of belief in story and discourse / by
Gillian Bennett.
        p. cm.
    New, expanded, and extensively rev. ed. of Traditions of belief, 1987.
    Includes bibliographical references.
    ISBN 0-87421-277-4 (pbk.)
    ISBN 0-87421-278-2 (cloth)
    1. Folklore—Great Britain. 2. Occultism—Great Britain. 3.
Ghosts—Great Britain. 4. Women—Great Britain—Folklore. I.
Traditions of belief. II. Title.
    GR141 .B55 1999
    398'.0941—dc21
                                                    99-6558
                                                    CIP

In Memoriam
Frederick George Lawley,
5 September 1916–26 March 1991

Contents

Introduction

Hamlet: *Alas, poor ghost!*
Ghost: *Pity me not/But lend thy serious*
    hearing/To what I shall unfold
                    Hamlet, *act 1, scene 5*

BACKGROUND

By successive stages folklorists have moved away from the idea that folklore is a body of old-fashioned leftovers from some shadowy pagan past which still survives among some special group called the "folk." They recognize too that, like every other body of knowledge from physics to philosophy, folklore may be true or it may be false, so they no longer subscribe to the popular definition that equates folklore with old wives' tales. Nevertheless, serious scholars remain very wary about studying *supernatural* folklore, so there is little opportunity to revise popular stereotypes or counteract educated prejudice.

Where it is not campaigned against by religious groups or sneered at by rationalists, the supernatural is often trivialized by the mechanisms of commerce. It has been taken over by TV, films, and ghost hunters in such a big way that shows and books can almost provide a classification system for popular notions about ghosts. So we find, for example, that ghosts may be allowed to exist on what we might call the "Scooby Doo" level, where they are either tameable or friendly or turn out to be frauds and fakes. They are also allowed existence on the "Haunted Inns of England" level, where they are regarded as tourist attractions, a specialty of the house, synthetic (and profitable) thrills. Alternatively, they may appear in "Stephen King" mode, where they are allowed to be threatening, but only to those deliberately seeking to be (safely and temporarily) threatened. So the supernatural has been officially demoted to the nursery, commercial, or fantasy worlds.

Yet people continue to have experiences which demand explanations that science as we define it today cannot provide; and they continue to need more than merely material things. Neither our formal culture nor our popular traditions can adequately meet these needs. People turn, therefore, to unofficial channels—to New Age beliefs or alternative religions perhaps; but more usually, to informal belief systems created and expressed through a network of interactions. They reinvent tradition through the folklore they offer each other in their personal experience stories, discussions, and exchanges of ideas.

At this informal level, there continues to be a very widespread belief in the supernatural. Many people still believe in poltergeists, fetches, wraiths, and warning ghosts, more or less as they did in the sixteenth and seventeenth centuries. There is also a heartfelt popular tradition that the souls of the family dead continue to exist somehow, somewhere, someway. Commentators who have claimed that supernatural belief is "obviously" much diminished in the Western world today have, I would suggest, been deceived by the official rationalist world view into not recognizing the existence of a rather different, unofficial one. When we know where to look and how to ask, it is easy to find plenty of evidence for the existence of a substantial supernatural folklore.

However, few folklorists have been prepared to enter this minefield. In Britain, only Andrew Lang (1844–1912) has had the courage and vision to challenge the dominant rationalist culture. His *Cock Lane and Common-Sense* (1894) is probably the best book on the subject written in the English language. It is in part a historical review of the history of ghost traditions, and in part an energetic argument that the evidence for ghosts is as good as the evidence for anything else. In succeeding generations of folklorists there have unfortunately been few to follow Lang's robust line. In Britain I can think of none. In America the record is rather better: the last forty years have produced a handful of scholars who have recognized the interest and value of studies of folk belief and have written about the supernatural without sneers or whimsicality. Among these, one should obviously mention Lynwood Montell and Wayland D. Hand (see especially Montell [1975] 1987; Hand 1976); but the name that principally comes to mind is David Hufford, whose work on "Old Hag" traditions resulted in the "experience-centered" approach to the study of folk belief (Hufford 1976, 1982a). Followers have adopted this approach and used it to triumphant effect in their own work (see especially the contributions to *Out of the Ordinary*, edited by Barbara Walker, and the special edition of *Western Folklore* "Reflexivity and the Study of Belief"). This approach also significantly influenced the doctoral thesis from which my *Traditions of Belief* was drawn (Bennett 1987), especially the notion that researchers should not disbelieve their informants on the basis of their own beliefs.

My work was also undertaken to explore the relationship between narrative and belief. For some time I had been uncomfortable with the commonplace assumption that legends are adequate guides to the nature of vernacular belief, so I wanted to put people in a position where they had to affirm or deny belief in an important, but controversial, matter and see how they responded. Would they tell stories—and, if so, what genre of stories would they tell? Nothing could be a more important but more disputed idea than that the dead can interact with the living; so it was this topic that I chose for my research. My plan was simple: to find a situation where I could conduct interviews, talk to people and ask them to answer a few questions about ghosts, and see what form their answers took. (Nothing, of course, is as simple as that: my fieldwork trials and errors are recounted in appendix 1.)

The studies that form the basis of the discussion in chapters 1, 2, and 4 below are based on material from this work, which was conducted during the 1980s in Manchester, a large commercial city in northwest England (see chapter 1 and appendix 1 for details).

It became obvious very early on in the original work that people do customarily respond to questions of belief with narrative answers. The more controversial the topic, the more likely it is that the conversation will include a lot of narrative. People who give positive answers in discussions about the supernatural are particularly likely to tell stories. These stories, however, are probably not legends in the sense of "traditional" legends. Most commonly they are records of personal experience, the narrator's own or that of a close friend or family member. The content is traditional, but the story text is almost always individual.

It is a matter of some debate what these sorts of informal personal stories should be called. There are those, among whom Linda Dégh is chief, who would argue that their traditional subject matter and their belief-related intention makes them "legends" and that our understanding of the legend genre should be expanded to include these little stories (see especially Dégh 1996). There was a time when I supported this view (Bennett 1989a). Now, however, I feel that this proposal neglects a useful distinction between, on the one hand, stories with traditional themes and motifs and a more or less traditional plot, and on the other, those that have a more or less traditional content but an idiosyncratic text.

Since the latter part of the 1970s—when Sandra Stahl triumphantly demonstrated that stories of personal experiences were a genuine folklore genre (1977)—many scholars have preferred to call these sorts of stories "personal narratives" (Roemer 1992), "personal experience narratives" (Gaudet 1992), or "experience narratives" (Butler 1990). Tantalizingly, however, these terms leave out any reference to just the features which the word "legend" highlights so well, and which are an important aspect of the sorts of stories I want to discuss here: their traditional motifs, their use in discussions about belief, and their supernatural content.

There is another word in common use—"memorates"— which, though not unproblematical (see Dégh and Vázsonyi 1974) is probably the least confusing of the available terms as far as the material in this book is concerned. Originally coined by the Swedish folklorist Carl von Sydow (1948) to refer to "purely personal" stories as opposed to the communal "fabulates," it points to the typical content and context of this sort of storytelling while at the same time indicating the individualness of the text. I have used it throughout this book to describe stories about supernatural events in which the narrator was the protagonist (or says she was), or which she witnessed (or says she did), or which were told to her by a confidante (or which she says were so told). The storytellers may use them to express either belief or disbelief, though belief will predominate.

A hundred years ago (perhaps even fifty years ago) a book on the folklore of British ghosts would have contained few, if any, memorates. Instead, it would have been a collection of more or less traditional legend texts about white ladies, boggarts, hauntings, and exorcisms. But the stories told and discussed here are very different: readers will not have heard them before, unless they happen to know the people who told them to me. They were told in the course of conversation—indeed they sometimes sound more like conversation than stories. They appear to be impromptu performances, and some may indeed have been unrehearsed, though others may have been told many times before.

Once recounted, supernatural experiences start to become subject to cultural processes. The event enters the public domain and social expectations are brought to bear on it. These include ideas about what constitutes both a "proper" experience of the supernatural and a "proper" ghost story. As Richard Bauman has pointed out, the relationship between story and event is reciprocal and works in both directions (1986, 52). Storytellers' and audiences' knowledge of what constitutes a proper supernatural event helps create the final shape of the stories that are told on the subject; conversely, knowledge of the stories is part of the shape we give to our supernatural experiences. In this sense stories are "applied folklore" (McEntire 1992, 82), or put another way, "stories structure the meanings by which a culture lives" (Cohan and Shires 1988, 1). So, though personal, these stories are also communal. They are embodiments of received attitudes and beliefs—tradition in action. They give meaning to meaningless perceptions, shape private experience into cultural forms, show how communal concepts are adapted to individual needs, and help create the very folklore they embody.

Stories such as these are the most effective way of showing what people actually believe or disbelieve. They save many paragraphs of explanation and discussion because they are more direct and vivid than any commentary can ever be. As Sir Philip Sidney said of the poet, so might we say of the teller of memorates:

> He beginneth not with obscure definitions, which must blur the margent with interpretations and must load the memory with doubtfulness; but he cometh to you

with words set in delightful proportion . . . and with a tale, forsooth, he cometh to you, with a tale which holdeth children from play, and old men from the chimney-corner. ([1598] 1959, 25)

THE STRUCTURE OF THIS BOOK

By way of a very broad contextualization, I have chosen to begin this book by looking at the way people's responses to tradition, experience, and memorates are shaped by cultural responses. After presenting the findings from the Manchester study, I focus on the way two intellectual traditions, the rationalist and supernaturalist, offer competing world views on which to base interpretations of experience. In chapter 2, I discuss the believers' memorates and the beliefs I think they encapsulate.

Some of the data discussed in chapter 3 is drawn from the Manchester material too, but most of it comes from a more recent study which was undertaken by my daughter, Dr. Kate Bennett, a gerontological psychologist at De Montfort University, Leicester, U.K. The research we discuss is part of a larger ongoing project on widows' and widowers' health, life-styles, and experiences (this is described in more detail in chapter 3 and appendix 1). At my request, she added a question about the "sense of presence," which is a very common feeling after a bereavement, to an early interview schedule. Chapter 3 is therefore a joint presentation. Together, we discuss the experience of bereavement and the sense of presence, which we believe are basic contexts for vernacular beliefs about personal contact with the dead. Chapter 4 returns to the data collected in Manchester, which I analyze to show how personal experience is transmuted into narrative form and shaped into philosophical debates between the narrator and an imaginary opponent. It seems to me that understanding the way stories like these are told is essential to understanding what they "mean." Without talking about the sort of negotiation that takes place in stories, we have only part of the picture of contemporary belief.

Finally, in chapter 5, I offer another contextualization of the material by looking at case studies in the history of supernatural beliefs. This chapter aims to be a glimpse of the historical context of modern conceptions, via the examination of three famous ghosts, the presentation of a famous debate between two interpretational traditions, and a history of belief in the power of the dead to witness and respond to the lives of the living.

The book is perhaps a little idiosyncratic by ending with extensive appendices. I have chosen to gather a variety of technical matters together in this way because, though I think they are important, I do not want them to intrude into the presentation of data which is otherwise personal and poignant. The book is therefore structured like a sandwich and side salad. The bread is represented by the contextualizing discussions of the first and final chapters; the filling is the central section that deals with beliefs and experiences of contact with the dead as recounted by contemporary urban women; the side salad is the appendices into which readers may dip as and when they choose. *Bon appétit.*

Gillian Bennett
October 1998

Chapter 1

Belief and Disbelief

IS BELIEF IN THE SUPERNATURAL DECLINING?

It is common nowadays to think that belief in the operation of supernatural forces is declining in the developed world. Historians and psychologists have hastened to assure us that "for the most part, the dead have little status or power in modern society" (Blauner 1966, 390), that "the social function of belief in ghosts is obviously much diminished and so is their extent" (Thomas 1971, 605), and that "ever since [the] age of enlightenment, percipients in . . . much of Western Europe, have attributed to the dead an ever-diminishing social role" (Finucane 1982, 222). Such statements betray a concept of history in which civilization is a process of movement (as they see it, "upward" movement) from a supernatural world view to a materialist one (or as they would term it, from superstition to rationality). There is no real evidence, however, for evolutionary assumptions as applied to society and culture, and there is certainly no evidence that rationalism and materialism are the evolutionary end point of civilization. So such statements may be based on no more than the prejudices of the authors and an assumption that the progression of society will *of course* lead towards abandoning belief in ghosts. One would like to see some evidence before accepting this point of view.

It must also be remembered that many or most writers have relied on written accounts for their portrait of supernatural beliefs. These may be literature, the classics, or local histories. Folklorists (also on the whole locked into the rationalist intellectual tradition) have compounded the impression by printing collections of readable but unbelievable legends and calling them the "folklore"

9

of the supernatural. If researchers rely solely on accounts like these, they get a very mixed bag of unlikely manifestations which defy belief. If they then ask people whether they believe in such things, of course they get negative answers. But that could simply mean that the researchers' own prejudices, or misinformation, has led them to ask the wrong questions. To find out what our contemporaries really believe, one must leave the books on one side and go out and try to access the informal oral traditions.

It would be wrong, however, to create the impression that this never happens. There have been several studies, though rather scattered and disparate. In 1926 a British national newspaper, the *Daily News*, invited readers to send in their personal experience accounts of ghosts. The result filled four volumes (one of which is still available in the Folklore Society library in London, see Giraud 1927). In the 1950s, British sociologist Geoffrey Gorer conducted a survey through a national newspaper for his *Exploring English Character*, which included questions about palm-reading, horoscopes and ghosts (1955). In 1968 and 1974 the Institute of Psychophysical Research appealed for firsthand reports of apparitions; approximately three hundred people responded to the first appeal, and fifteen hundred to the second (Green and McCreery 1975). More recently, the Department of Sociology at Leeds University conducted a study into what they call "common" religion (folklorists would call it "folk" religion, or perhaps "vernacular" religion—see Primiano, 1995). They asked questions, among other things, about life after death, ghosts, telepathy, clairvoyance, fortune-telling, and horoscopes (Towler et al. 1981–84). More recently, extensive survey work has been undertaken by anthropologist and theologian Douglas Davies into popular attitudes towards all aspects of death and burial. Two of his surveys in particular have provided very useful information about popular attitudes to supernatural traditions. These are the Rural Churches Project, the report of which was published in 1990 (Davies, Watkins, and Winter 1991), and a very much larger survey of 1,603 individuals (Davies and Shaw 1995). In Switzerland, in 1954–55, the popular fortnightly *Schweizer Beobachter* initiated an enquiry into prophetic dreams, coincidences, premonitions, and apparitions, and received fifteen hundred accounts (Jaffé 1979).

In the U.S., Louis C. Jones surveyed young Americans and included an account of their responses in his very readable *Things That Go Bump in the Night* (1959). In the 1970s a couple of questions about psychic experiences were included in a survey of basic belief systems commissioned by the Henry Luce Foundation, and 1,460 replies were obtained (Greeley 1975). Two researchers at the School of Public Health, UCLA, interviewed 434 people from four ethnic groups in greater Los Angeles asking them had they "ever experienced or felt the presence of anyone after he had died?" (Kalish and Reynolds 1973). Also in the 1970s, two very important collections of local ghostlore were published, William Lynwood Montell's *Ghosts along the Cumberland: Deathlore in the Kentucky Foothills* ([1975] 1987) and Ray B. Browne's *"A Night with the Hants" and Other Alabama Folk Experiences* (1976). In the fall of 1986, *The Skeptical Inquirer* printed a survey of "pseudoscientific beliefs about the past" among college students (see Harrold and Eve 1986, table 1, p. 67). A study of "Paranormal Experiences in the General Population" in the psychiatric *Journal of Nervous and Mental Disease* surveyed a random sample of 502 people in Winnipeg, Canada (Ross and Joshi 1992) .

One consistent conclusion from all this research is that popular belief in supernatural cause and effect is higher than one would have thought possible in predominantly rationalist cultures and that it has been consistently underestimated. In the U.S., Richard Kalish and David Reynolds obtained an average of 44 percent positive answers to their "presence" question (1973); Francis Harrold and Raymond Eve found that 35 percent of people thought "ghosts exist," 59 percent believed some people could "predict the future by psychic power," 38 percent thought "communication with the dead is possible," and 67 percent believed "heaven exists" (1986, table 1, p. 67); and Colin Ross and Shaun Joshi found that 15.6 percent of their respondents claimed experiences of telepathy and 5.8 percent of precognition; 5.2 percent had had contact with ghosts, 2.2 percent with poltergeists and 4.4 percent with other spirits (1992 [the results were attributed to dissociative disorders]; and see David Hufford's reply [1992]). Andrew Greeley found that the "majority" of his American sample had had some sort of psychic experience, and a "respectable proportion" had had them frequently. Twenty-seven percent of his sample reported they had had contact with the dead, 3 percent saying this was a frequent occurrence (1975). In the U.K., Geoffrey Gorer found that 30 percent of his respondents believed in palm reading, 20 percent in astrology, and 17 percent in ghosts (1955); Celia Green and Charles McCreery found that "about a third" of their respondents reported having seen an apparition (1975, viii); and the Leeds team found that 14 percent of their respondents believed in astrology, 35 percent in fortune-telling, 36 percent in ghosts, 54 percent in clairvoyance, and 61 percent in telepathy (Krarup 1982). Davies's survey for the Rural Churches Project not only found a range of beliefs in an afterlife, but discovered that 19 percent of Anglicans and 29 percent of other denominations believed in ghosts (1997, 156). The survey also uncovered substantial evidence that a significant proportion of the population (just under half of the people surveyed) believed they "had gained some sort of experience which they believed involved an encounter or communication with a dead person." Commenting on this, Davies added: "By and large they involve a sense of presence . . . but for a significant minority the visitation is visual . . . on some rare occasions a voice is heard or some sort of communication is felt to take place." "Far from being secular," one British scholar of religion has noted, "our culture wobbles between a partially absorbed Christianity biased towards comfort and the need for confidence, and beliefs in fate, luck and moral governance incongruously joined together" (Martin 1967, 76).

My own study conducted in Manchester (U.K.) confirms these findings. The information was collected from women who attended my father's podiatrist clinic in the 1980s. Over the five-month period I worked there, I interviewed a total of 132 people—13 men, 3 women between eighteen and twenty-five years old, 20 women from age forty to sixty, and 96 women over sixty. From these I selected a study group of 87 whom I knew, or judged, to be over sixty years old. I was not able to find out the age and domestic circumstances of 6 of these women. Of the other 81, 29 were between ages sixty and seventy (of whom 6 were single, 14 married, and 9 widowed); 44 were between ages seventy and eighty (of whom 9 were single, 10 married and 25 were widowed); 8 were age eighty and over (of whom one was single, 2 were married, and 5 were widowed); the eldest lady was ninety-six. Forty-three of them lived alone, the rest lived with family or friends. Most of the respondents said they were church-goers or professed some sort of religious conviction/adherence. A small minority were Jewish; the majority were Christians, with Methodists predominating and a handful each of Anglicans, Presbyterians and Roman Catholics; only one professed to be an atheist. Unless otherwise stated, all illustrative material is drawn from interviews with these 87 women. Readers will find a little basic biographical information about each one in appendix 3.

As a guide to the way I wanted conversation to develop, I compiled a checklist of topics around which to focus questions and discussion. Originally it had been my intention to encourage talk only about the possibility of interaction between the dead and the living, but in practice I found that this was far too intimidating, so I widened the scope of my research to include less alarming and delicate matters—extrasensory perception, omens, premonitions, fortune-telling and horoscopes, and the possibility of life after death. In practice, I usually began with questions about horoscopes or life after death and worked round to the more difficult matters as and when I could. I even asked questions about life on other planets if I felt that the respondent needed a long run-in to the topic. Conversely, I found that questions about telepathy made a convenient exit point when the patient's treatment was drawing to a close. Though it had not been my original intention to do any research in these areas, in the end I was very glad that I had done so, because I came to believe that all these subjects form a sort of background or context to more serious beliefs. It also gave me responses on a wide range of topics that are likely to come up in discourse with others and gave me a point of comparison with previous studies.

The women's scores on all the "deeper" and more delicate topics were very high, even higher than previous studies suggested. Almost two-thirds of the 87 women said they believed that some sort of contact with the dead was possible; nearly half with conviction and several others with only slightly less certainty. They were less likely, however, to believe in poltergeists and haunting ghosts, though even here the figure was higher than might have been expected (some expressing convinced belief, others thinking the phenomenon possibly really occurs, yet others speaking in this context about "happy" or "unhappy" houses).[1] In addition, a large proportion of them said they thought it was possible to be fore-warned that "something's going to happen"; nearly half of them were *certain* of it and believed themselves to be "a little bit psy-chic." Even more believed in omens of death—mysterious noises, the scent of flowers, broken mirrors, dreams,[2] visions, and so on—and half of them could cite personal examples. Slightly fewer were convinced telepathy was possible, though many of them had expe-rienced it themselves. Several others thought it was at least likely, and only a minority thought it did not and could not occur. The results are given in graphic form below on pages 19–23.

It must be stressed that these women were not ignorant or ill-educated; nor were they socially or geographically isolated. They were dignified, sensible, experienced women, living in a middle-class suburb in a large city. Neither were they in any way eccentric; on the contrary, they were pillars of their church and local com-munity, essentially "respectable" in even the narrowest sense of that unpleasant term. Figures such as these do not at all give the impression that belief in supernatural cause and effect is declining. It would seem that the world view of quite a substantial proportion of the population is probably decidedly less materialistic than sci-entists and historians imagine.

Telling It Slant

One of the many problems of any research into supernatural beliefs is the slipperiness of language and the fact that people often want to express themselves with face-saving ambiguity. In Emily Dickinson's phrase, they "tell the truth but tell it slant." Under these circumstances, it is easy for researchers to misunderstand or misrepresent the views of their respondents.

The first sort of unwitting error is to ask a question in such a way as to get a misleading result. In my own fieldwork, for exam-ple, I found that the choice of terminology was crucial. I quickly found out that I had to adapt the wording of my questions and prompts to fit in with the phraseology the women themselves used.

"Alas, Poor Ghost!"

For example, terms like "supernatural" had to be abandoned altogether; for my informants, it was not the neutral nor factual term it is for me—its connotations were wholly evil and taboo. As long as I said I was doing research on "the supernatural," I had only negative reactions, ranging from denial to hostility and even real fear. As soon as I took to speaking in vague fashion about "the mysterious side of life," people relented; they began to show decided interest and were eager to talk. Similarly, when I started out, I had simply followed the practice of sociologist Geoffrey Gorer (1955) and blankly asked, "Do you believe in ghosts?" And everybody had promptly said, "No." Luckily, I was soon put on the right track by a woman who said she didn't believe in ghosts, but she knew that a house could be "spirited" and in fact she had once lived in a house that "wasn't right." On the same day, an old lady said she didn't believe in ghosts, but "funnily enough, whenever someone's going to be ill in my family, my mother comes TO me." Following these linguistic clues, from then on I talked about "*things* in houses" and experiences where dead parents and husbands "come to" the living. Douglas Davies and his colleagues similarly had to adapt their terminology for the Rural Churches Project. Discussing their attempts to frame a meaningful question about reincarnation, Davies remarks: "It may be that those using the word do so by placing their own meaning upon it . . . . Accordingly, we decided that the expression 'coming back as something or someone else' would be more meaningful" (1997, 150). Formal surveys and written questionnaires do not allow this sort of negotiation and so are fertile ground for misrepresentation. This may be one of the reasons why the strength of the belief tradition is consistently underestimated.

A second sort of misrepresentation may occur when writers wedded to the rationalist culture discuss their findings. Here, I believe Davies errs in the way he presents his evidence. Chapter 10 of his *Death, Ritual and Belief* (1997) deals with "Souls and the Presence of the Dead" in an eminently readable and enlightening way, but plainly from within the rationalist tradition, as his choice of words reveals. For example, he constantly uses phrases like "when people *reckon to have* seen the dead" (my emphasis). Approximately 35 percent of his Rural Churches sample, he says, had had "some sense of the presence of the dead." This experience he divides into visitations, "physical and auditory awareness," dreams, "the dead in living memory," and "talking to the dead." Many of the people he quotes also speak of experiences which they say were "almost real." As far as one can tell, all these are included in the 35 percent who have at some time been aware of the presence of the dead, but the effect of dealing with "dreams" and "talking to the dead" separately from "visitations" and "physical and auditory awareness" is nevertheless misleading because these experiences may actually be very similar. It could very well be only the respondents' choice of words or the writer's decision about what "really" happened that differentiate them, not the nature of the experience. A personal story may be in order here. After the death of my father-in-law, his second wife whom he married late in life told me that one night she came downstairs and "dreamt" she saw him standing by the dining room sideboard, and that she put her hand on his heart and felt it beating. When she repeated the story to my mother, however, she told it as a real experience, not as a dream. The factor that altered the story was the audience to whom it was told; nothing else had changed. A similar phenomenon has been noted by Edgar Slotkin in his study of "Legend Genre as a Function of Audience" (1988).

The women in the Manchester study group routinely used a range of expressions to discuss their experiences. References to "dreams" and "dreaming," phrases such as "it was as if . . . ," "I felt as if . . . ," and "it was almost as if . . ." were used alongside phrases that apparently record quite different experiences, but were in fact used more or less interchangeably—"I saw him quite plainly," and so on. Sometimes a speaker would switch from one to the other in the same narrative. In the story which introduces chapter 3, for example, the narrator switches from "I was fully awake" and "he stood in front of me" to "I don't know whether I was dreaming or not," and back to "and he was there" within the course of a single narrative. There are many explanations for these switches—familiarity with both rationalist and supernaturalist interpretational frameworks, greater or lesser awareness of audience, and so on—but the point is that the language of "dreams" and "as if" should not be taken too literally. In most cases, a safer guide can be found in linguistic clues picked up in recordings and interviews. Sometimes these are quite subtle. For example, partial belief is often indicated by a phrase such as "not REALLY, but . . ." and a partially skeptical attitude by "I don't think so, REALLY." These expressions seem remarkably similar until you take word order, tempo, and intonation into account. When expressing some measure of belief, for example, a speaker will usually pause after the word "really," but when she is slightly skeptical she pauses before it. Her intonation is slightly different too: when she almost believes, the word "really" will be spoken with a slightly rising intonation, but when she almost disbelieves her voice will tend to fall. There are linguistic and paralinguistic clues, too, for outright skepticism and outright belief. These are discussed in more detail in appendix 4. (To interpret transcription techniques, refer to the conventions discussed in appendix 2.)

PATTERNS OF BELIEF

When discussing the effect of language, it is interesting in this connection to note that only evil manifestations were called "ghosts" by the Manchester women, and that they seldom used the word "spirit" except in the context of "evil spirits." Terms commonly used in academic discourse for neutral or beneficent encounters—"apparition," "revenant"—were hardly ever used, which gives the researcher a terminological problem. In the bar graphs below, and in the remainder of this book, therefore, I have chosen to resolve this dilemma by referring to these sorts of encounter as "visitations." The terms "ghost" and "haunting" will be reserved for threatening encounters.

The graphs show that the Manchester women were highly likely to accept traditional beliefs about visitations from the dead, premonitions, omens, and telepathy. Rather fewer of them (though still a significant proportion) also believed in "ghosts" and "hauntings." When fortune-telling and astrology were discussed, however, the picture changed. Here, the skeptics were numerically stronger. It is certainly curious that many who were happy to profess belief in omens, premonitions, and the return of the dead were reluctant to give credit to beliefs that one might have thought were more acceptable and less extreme manifestations of a supernaturalist world view.

I have discussed the women's beliefs about premonitions and fortune-telling in my chapter in Barbara Walker's *Out of the Ordinary* (Bennett 1995) and intend to focus in this book solely on beliefs relating to contact with the dead, but something has to be said here about this curious turnabout. Discussing afterlife beliefs, Davies writes:

> Beliefs can be held, and probably usually are held, in cluster-form rather than in a systematic scheme . . . various beliefs which may have no immediate logical or theological connection with each other are brought together to give the individual a working basis for life. Such beliefs, held in bundles together, may even appear contradictory if spelled out and analysed logically. (1997, 151)

There is some truth in that, of course, and to an extent that appears to be happening in this case. However, I believe there is a logic to this apparently contradictory position.

By listening to all the conversation recorded on the interview tapes, it is possible to pick up a very good general picture of the mental furniture the women carry round with them, and this is most instructive when trying to understand the whys and wherefores of belief. Judging from this background information, it seems that philosophical considerations and social factors are influential in determining *whether* women accept supernatural traditions (see below), but it is moral factors that are most significant in distinguishing between *which* traditions they accept and which they do not. The Manchester study group members were elderly, conventional, churchgoing, and very much geared to traditional roles and pursuits. Their beliefs and attitudes were bound to be influenced by considerations of morality, and their morality by received ideals of the relationships of women to men, individuals to society, and mankind to God. Like it or not, these women were taught by the society they grew up in that the ideal member of their sex is an intuitive, gentle, unassertive person, geared to a caring and supportive role rather than to direct action, independent thought, or concern with self. Whether a particular traditional belief was

Percentage of belief and disbelief in eight topics
(rounded to nearest whole percent)
as expressed by the Manchester women

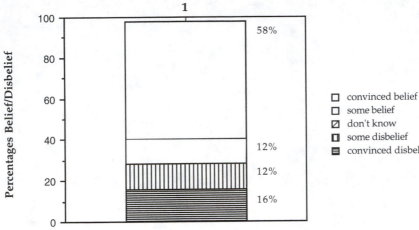

Life After Death

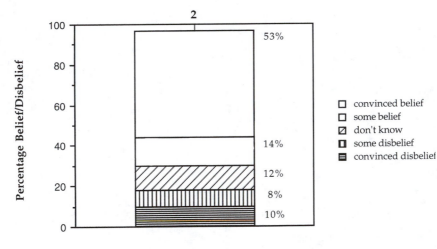

Telepathy

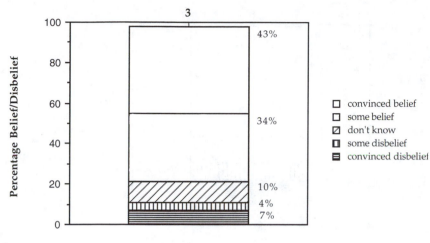

Premonitions

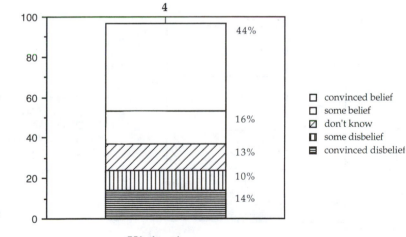

Visitations

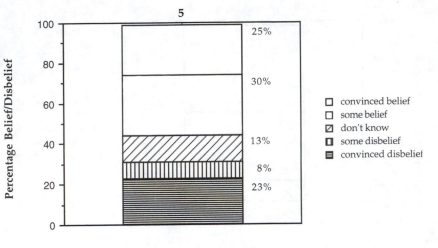

5

25%

30%

13%

8%

23%

- ☐ convinced belief
- ☐ some belief
- ▨ don't know
- ▥ some disbelief
- ▤ convinced disbelief

Omens of Death

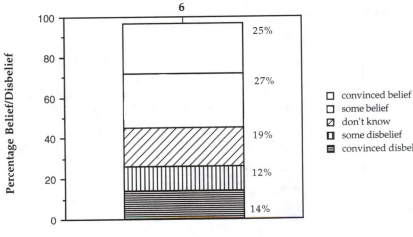

6

25%

27%

19%

12%

14%

- ☐ convinced belief
- ☐ some belief
- ▨ don't know
- ▥ some disbelief
- ▤ convinced disbelief

Hauntings

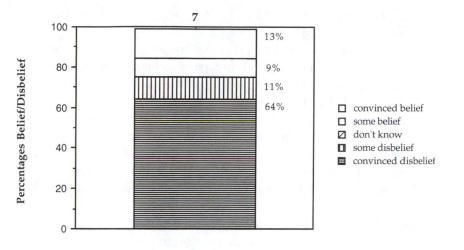

7

Fortunetelling

- convinced belief
- some belief
- don't know
- some disbelief
- convinced disbelief

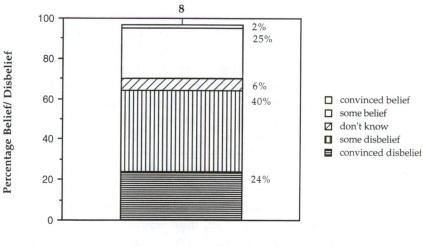

8

Horoscopes

- convinced belief
- some belief
- don't know
- some disbelief
- convinced disbelief

acceptable to them seemed to be to a large extent dependent on these basic assumptions.

It is very possible that premonitions and telepathy scored so highly on their belief scale because, par excellence, they are seen as intuitions which come unsought, not as the result of the active pursuit of knowledge. They turn outwards from the self to the immediate circle of family and friends. They are love of others made manifest, defeated by neither time nor distance, and felt in the deep recesses of the heart where none may challenge their authority. In contrast, fortune-telling and astrology are intellectual pursuits—a learned ability to interpret purely material signs, deliberately sought experiences which effectively devalue intuition. In addition, they are self-centered, not other-person-oriented. It is a woman's own fortune that is told, and her own fate that is read in the stars; other people are thrust into the role of supporting cast and she steps center-stage.

Similarly, the women were much more likely to say that they believed in visitations than in ghosts. As they described it, they were made aware of the dead more often through sensing their presence than by seeing them in physical form. When a dead mother "comes to" her distressed daughter, she comes unbidden and her presence is evidence of mutual caring, proof that other-person-centeredness works even from beyond the grave. In contrast, a person who hears mysterious footsteps in the attic, or witnesses doors opening of their own accord, or sees apparitions of unknown people passing up the stairs is surrounded by a world of *strangers*, where intruders creep even into the heart of the family and invade the circle round the hearth.

These are patterns which appeared over and over again as the women described their beliefs and experiences. To a very large extent, the degree of belief that was in general accorded to any supernatural concept could be predicted by its position on four continua from intuitive to objective, from unsought to sought, from interpersonal to selfish, and from safe to dangerous. So, whereas nearly two-thirds of the women believed in visitations from the good dead, and still more believed in premonitions and telepathy (all intuitive, unsought, interpersonal happenings that encourage a feeling that the world is safe), scarcely more than a quarter had much belief in astrology and fortune-telling (acquired skills or deliberately sought, self-centered experiences that introduce an element of the unknown into ordinary living). It seems, then, that the acceptability of a supernatural construct depends to a large extent on its morality in the women's eyes and, in turn, that this morality is dependent on their perception of a woman's "proper" role and social persona and their need to see the world as an orderly, harmonious sphere for God's goodness and human affection.

Order in Chaos

One of the primary values the Manchester women shared was the concept of order. I think it may be the different way she seeks to find order in the chaos of life that determines whether a particular woman favors a materialistic or supernaturalistic world view.

One way of responding to the unpredictability of life events and the oddities of human experience is to adopt a view of the world as governed by unrevealed laws. If this is a woman's preferred strategy, she will say:

- The world's a great study and a great puzzle. (Elisabeth)

- There are more things in heaven and earth than we dream of. (Rose)

- The world's so wonderful, isn't it? And we just don't know what there is. (Violet)

- There is far more to know than we are ready for yet. (Kathleen)

- It's such a beautiful, wonderful universe, anything is possible. (Margot)

This philosophy may take a religious form, in which case the world is seen as driven by divine providence and therefore not random, however incapable it is of being understood. Alternatively, it may take a mystical form, in which case the world is seen as full of magic and wonders. Many of the women claimed to be "a little bit psychic" and several said that they had been offered the chance to train as mediums (a chance all had turned down, so they said). The dominant impression was that the psychic powers they claimed were correlations of, or substitutes for, conventional religion. Both religion and mysticism gain for their adherents a relaxed acceptance of life's oddities and the chaos of the material world, allowing them to control disorder by reinterpreting it as unrevealed order.

Alternatively, it is possible to impose order on life by ignoring or denying disorder. The religious form of this strategy may take the form of presupposing an immutable divine plan—life is a machine which God has set in motion and which, once running, cannot be stopped or altered:

- You see, I'm a practising Christian and that makes me believe that "What is to be, will be." (Dora)

- When God wants you, you'll go. He'll take you and that's it. (Norah)

This may take a secular form as a sort of grim fatalism, according to which one's feet have been set on one's lifetime path at birth and there can be no turning aside:

- My father used to say that from the moment you're born to the moment you die, your life is mapped out for you. He says NOTHING will alter it. (Evelyn)

- I think what will be, will be. That's my opinion. (Polly)

- I think that what happens to you, just happens, you know. I think that if fate means you to have it, well it just happens. (Constance)

- I think your days are planned for you. No point in trying to find out. (Iris)

Others may adopt an "ignorance is strength" philosophy—refusing to think about chance and disorder at all. They describe themselves as "not fanciful," or "a day-to-day person," or rather reproachfully say that they "don't GO IN for" fortune-telling and horoscopes, or they "don't BELIEVE in it," in the sense of not *approving* of it, or they "don't want to KNOW about it." Obviously, this attitude owes a lot to the Eden myth, but underneath the piety there might also be a bit of superstition—as if knowledge itself had malicious power to harm.

In other answers, we can get a glimpse of the sort of anxiety which may perhaps be an underlying factor in the rejection of the supernatural:

- It wouldn't do for me to think too deeply because I'd get too upset. You think, "Oh no! I must keep out of that!" (Thora)

- I'm a day-to-day person, and if it comes, it comes. But I mean, if somebody says to me they thought something was going to happen, I would be so worried, so ill. I'm better not knowing. (Dolly)

- There was a time when I got really hooked, until I realized the state I'd got into with it and I just had to try and stop myself reading it [daily horoscope]. I was looking for the bad things to happen. (Marjorie)

Significantly, too, many skeptics are inclined to feel that, though they disbelieve (and need to disbelieve), they could be persuadable, given the right conditions:

- I think I'm skeptical really. Until probably if anything happened to ME. Then it might be a different THING. (Doreen)

- I don't know, but if there WAS a ghost in a house, I wouldn't go and live in it! (Cora)

So when the topic of discussion turns to "deep" matters, these two philosophies guide their adherents either to the supernaturalist or the rationalist tradition. Only a few of the Manchester women crossed sides and gave "rational" answers to some of these sorts of questions and "supernaturalist" to others, and only seventeen of them reversed their position. On the whole, a woman who believed that contact with the dead is possible also believed in most forms of divination and precognition. Similarly, women who disbelieved in contact with the dead also discounted extrasensory perception and related matters.

Family Love

There is another thing that seems to significantly contribute to whether a woman will believe or disbelieve that visitations from the dead are possible—that is the social situation of the individual person—but it does not work in quite the way one would expect. One would imagine that factors such as ageing, widowhood, and solitude would be of paramount significance, or that fear of death would lead the elderly to a search for immortality. However, though these suppositions seem obvious, they were not borne out in the Manchester study. I found that readiness to believe did not increase with age in any fixed progression and was not more observable in widows and those who lived alone than among married people. It seems to be sociability itself—interest in others, and especially love of family—that most often predisposes women towards belief.

One simple way of showing this is by comparing the incidence of belief among women to whom kinship and friendship were obviously important with that among women with apparently much less family feeling or interest in others. When listening to the tapes I recorded, about half the women stood out as being "family women." All their talk, whatever its ostensible subject, was sprinkled with references to dead and living members of the clan—aunts and unles, nieces and nephews, parents and grandparents. Others, whom I thought of as "social women," talked a good deal about friends, though not about family; and others were simply voluble and discursive (I thought of them as "talkers"). Altogether, there were 42 "family women," 5 "social women," 11 "talkers," and 29 who could not be described in any of these ways. What is interesting—and I think significant—is that the incidence of belief in supernatural traditions seems to decline proportionally with these social factors, especially as the "family" factor is diluted. Among "family women" it stood at 83 percent; among "family women" and "social women" taken together it was 78 percent; among "family women," "social women," and "talkers" taken as a single group, it further declined to 66 percent. Among women who fitted none of these categories—and might be assumed to be either more isolated or less socially aware—it was lowest of all. Only 27.5 percent of such women expressed any belief, and 58.6 percent strenuously denied it. It appears, therefore, that social factors may be important in predisposing some people to belief in the continued presence and influence of the dead, and that perhaps the single most significant aspect of these social parameters may be devotion to family and family life. There is evidence that women who put a high value on personal relationships will be reluctant to give them up even when death intervenes, and that they see the relationships of mutual love—parent and child, husband and wife—continuing even when one of the partners is dead.

The same would seem to have held true for several centuries. Fr. Noel Taillepied, for example, writing in 1588 said that a ghost "will naturally, if it is possible, appear to the person whom he has most loved whilst on earth, since this person will be readiest to carry out any behest or fulfil any wish then communicated by the departed" (n.d., 95). Arguments for the importance of settled family life in the establishment of ghost traditions may also be found in Keith Thomas's great work, *Religion and the Decline of Magic* (1971, 602), and it has long been assumed that ghost belief flourishes best in settled communities (though these are often assumed to be rural communities). British sociologist Joan Rockwell noted in her work on Danish folklorist Evald Tang Kristensen:

> I would venture a speculation that belief in ghosts can only be a significant part of a culture where long-continued intensive agriculture makes a continuity both of habitation and of human family generations possible. It is to the established family hearth that the ancestors return to give advice and warning. (1981, 43)

The major relevance is not location, I believe, but love for the dead person and respect for family life.

Robert Blauner, in an often quoted article in the journal *Psychiatry*, wherein he attempts to account for what he sees as the demise of ghost belief today, discusses this question. Comparing modern societies to "traditional" ones, he argues that "when people die who are engaged in vital functions of society . . . their importance cannot be easily reduced . . . . Ghosts are reifications of this unfinished business, and belief in their existence may permit some continuation of relationships broken off before their natural terminus" (1966, 381). He demonstrates, from anthropological research, how in many areas of the world the early death of important members of the family results in ghost traditions. Then he goes on to argue that

> the relative absence of ghosts in modern society is not simply a result of the routing of superstition by science and rational thought, but also reflects the disengaged social situation of the majority of the deceased. In a society where the young and middle-aged have largely liberated themselves from the authority of and emotional dependence upon old people by the time of the latter's death, there is little social-psychological need for a vivid community of the dead. (1966, 382)

Here, of course, he not only reveals his prejudices through his choice of words—"superstition," "rational thought," "liberated"— but also displays the weakness of his argument as it applies to modern society. It is a distortion to speak of the young and middle-aged as having "liberated" themselves from dependence on the old. People need their families for emotional support whatever age they are or whatever country they live in; and to say that today the elderly have no authority is a cliché for which there is no real evidence. Elderly males still dominate the political scene in many developed countries. Mothers still retain a good deal of influence over their grown-up children, especially their daughters. The memorates the Manchester women told me show time and again that the importance of families, especially mothers and husbands, "cannot be easily reduced," and that this is (justly) interpreted as love, not slavery. Close family members cannot be replaced and the dead are still needed (that's the nature of bereavement, as we shall see in chapter 3). Blauner's analysis of the reasons for the prevalence of ghosts in traditional societies holds equally well for advanced societies, I believe, and is the context for many of the experiences discussed in this book.

COMPETING CULTURES

Contemporary Western culture offers two contrasting sets of expectations and explanations to choose from—rationalist "traditions of disbelief"; and a supernaturalist culture, the "traditions of belief" that are the subtitle of this book. Here, for example, is Vanessa,[3] an eighty-year-old widow, struggling to find an answer to a question about the power of the dead to return to this world:[4]

- Well, I have SEEN my mother sometimes— occasionally. But whether that's occasions that she's been on my mind or something—
  [G. B.: How did you come to see your mother? Did she—?]
  It was in the night. Whether I was dreaming about her I don't know. I saw her quite plainly. It only happened once to me. But whether she was on my mind or not I don't know, and I can't remember whether perhaps I was a bit low.
  [G. B.: How long ago was this, Vanessa?]
  Oh, I can't say how long.
  [G. B.: When you were younger?]
  No, the last few years. And it just came over me whether it was a warning that I WAS going to meet her or something. I never said anything to anybody about it.

Vanessa plainly cannot entirely decide, or will not say, whether what she saw was objective or subjective. Two traditions are available to her as explanatory mechanisms, and she hovers between the two. On the one hand, she uses the language of supernatural belief ("I have SEEN my mother," "I saw her quite plainly") and relies on some of the traditional assumptions about the reasons why the dead may contact the living which we will meet in chapter 2 ("And it just came over me whether it was a warning that I WAS going to meet her"). On the other hand, she uses explanatory concepts drawn from the rationalist tradition; she wonders whether she was dreaming or whether it happened because "she's been on my mind or something" or because she was feeling "a bit low."

In the following, and final, sections of this chapter I want to look at these competing cultures, both in general and as they are reflected in the replies that the Manchester women gave to my enquiries.

Traditions of Disbelief

The term "traditions of disbelief" was first used by David Hufford in an important article of 1982, but just less than a hundred years previously that other great "psycho-folklorist,"[5] Andrew Lang, summed up the arguments used by rationalists in remarkably similar terms:

> On every side we find in all ages, climates, races and stages of civilization, consentient testimony to a set of extraordinary phenomena, but we are bullied by common-sense into accepting feeble rationalizations. . . . When we ask for more than "all stuff and nonsense," we speedily receive a very mixed theory in which rats, indigestion, dreams, and, of late, hypnotism, are mingled much at random. (Lang 1894, 173)

To this list, Hufford adds psychological desires, the need to control children, mind-altering drugs, alcohol, delirium, stress, and psychosis. At the last ditch, rationalists fall back on the argument that, even if none of their arguments will fit the case now, given time and the advance of scientific knowledge, a "rational" cause *will eventually be found* (Hufford 1982b).

How far all this reasoning is traditional may be illustrated by the fact that very much the same sort of arguments may be found in old texts. For example, in *Of Ghosts and Spirits Walking by Night* the Swiss Protestant, Lewes (Ludowig) Lavater, writing in the second half of the sixteenth century, proposed to demonstrate that "Melancholike persons and madde men, imagine things which in very deed are not," "Fearfull menne, imagine that they see and heare straunge things," and "Men which are dull of seeing and hearing imagine many things which in very deede are not so." He also discusses tricks used to scare children into obedience, jokes and pranks played by young men, and legends and tales. He proposes that some supernatural encounters are deliberate deceptions, and argues that "Manye naturall things are taken to bee ghosts" (Lavater [1572] 1929, contents list). It is customary to see only believers as adhering to established traditional patterns of thought and having a "folklore," but it seems that the rationalists' "explanations" are just as traditional. Rationalists, too, have folklore.

The rationalist folklore was very observable among some of the Manchester women. At its most extreme, the culture of disbelief was maintained by making derogatory assertions about people who have reported supernatural experiences. They were said to be confused, emotional, muddled, or manipulative. They:

- . . . have put the wrong interpretation on it. (Colette)

- . . . are probably very highly strung and imaginative. (Dorothy)

- . . . are doing that just for the publicity. (Stella)

- . . . are doing it just to get a new house. (Doris)

- . . . are people whose emotions are very charged. (Doreen)

Also,

- when people are very bad with their nerves, they think all sorts of things! (Enid)

Elsewhere, they attempt, as it were, to reason with the supernaturalist tradition:

- No! Because nobody's come back to tell you. (Constance)

- Well, I've never had any experience of anything like that. (Zena)

- Well it's never been known up to now, has it? (Cora).

- Nobody's come back, have they? (Evelyn)

- No, because you must go back thousands of years, mustn't you? Well, I mean, if people are going to come back from all those years, well I can't see how it can be! (Gwen)

- They never come back at a seance and tell you anything worthwhile. (Hilda)

- I have a theory that you're put on this earth for so long and that's your span of life. It's like a flower. A flower dies—another one doesn't grow in its place, you've got to plant something else, haven't you? (Paula)

- No, as far as I'm concerned, once you're dead you're dead. Look at the animals for that. (Rita)

- I think with the body's death—I don't think about the soul because nobody knows whether we've got a soul— I think our bodies die like the plants and flowers do. (Phyllis)

Where they have to face popular opinion at first hand and respond to acquaintances who report subjective experiences such as the "feeling of presence" that will be discussed in chapter 3, the occurrences are often attributed to the power of dreams and desire, or to the influence of past associations:

- My mother still thinks of him so much (of her son so much) that she sometimes does come down in the morning and say he was in the room with her, but, you know, whether that's half dreaming or not, it's hard to say. (Doreen)

- I think that is rather involved in one's teaching from childhood and when there is distress or any other crisis we probably revert to what we've been taught and go over it again. That's how I think I'd explain that. (Bessie)

- I think one might feel that one has been helped by thinking about them, but whether any actual spirit comes to help you I should rather doubt. I think it's more INSIDE YOU. You get the comfort and strength from contact with whoever it is that you're thinking of rather than that they come specially to help you, in the spirit or any other way. (Rina)

- Well, I think you live through your parents a lot during your life. Personally I think an awful lot of the way you were brought up and the things they say as regards religion and everything does stay with you and you tend to talk about it at times. (Doris)

Similar arguments structure their discourse about other issues that were discussed in the interviews, such as fortune-telling, omens, and premonitions. As far as fortune-telling is concerned, these take the form of arguing that any correspondence between prediction and outcome is coincidence, or that recourse to a clairvoyant is merely superstitious, or irrelevant because the future is "in the Maker's hands," or, most commonly, a neat argument that the skill of the clairvoyant lies more in her ability to "react to your reactions" than to any genuine psychic powers. When the women move on to discuss omens and premonitions, the ready-made counterarguments are more numerous. Apart from having obvious objections such as that these beliefs are superstitious, open to religious objections, and deceptive, skeptical women assert that such notions are "fanciful," or "sheer imagination," or use other such generalized rebuttals. In addition, they employ sophisticated arguments which counter belief in detail as well as substance. Such strange feelings and mood changes are "really" due to a variety of natural causes—unconscious anxiety, low spirits, poor health, atmospheric conditions. Precognitive dreams are explained as chance reshapings of the previous day's events (and thus in no *need* of explanation, supernatural or otherwise).

Traditions of Belief

Countering this rationalist folklore are the traditional supernaturalist arguments (which I call "traditions of belief"). These are commonly based on human testimony, on evidence drawn from personal experience, and the stories of friends and relatives (whose veracity, rationality, and sobriety are earnestly vouched for). Discussants also point out that both religion and tradition are firmly in favor of the continued existence of the souls of the dead, and that there is empirical testimony that they do interact with living people.

Again, this is wholly traditional reasoning. In a report of a famous seventeenth-century poltergeist case which occurred at the home of a certain Mr. Mompesson, for example, the author summed up his case as follows:

> Mr Mompesson is a Gentleman, of whose truth in this account I have not the least suspicion, he being neither vain nor credulous, but a discreet, sagacious and manly person. Now the credit of matters of Fact depends much upon the relators who, if they cannot be deceived themselves, nor supposed anyways interested to impose upon others, ought to be credited. For upon these circumstances, all Human faith is grounded, and matter of Fact is not capable of any proof beside but immediate sensible [that is, "sensory"] evidence. (Glanvil 1681, 83)

Unlike the skeptics whose case is ultimately based on the assumption that people not only are frequently misled themselves but also do indeed sometimes want to mislead others, believers have faith in human perception and trust other people to see accurately and interpret correctly what happens in the world around them. It is the interaction of tradition, "news," rumors, and written accounts with personal experience that forms the basis of their case.

The arguments are never slick, though, the respondents customarily expressing sincere puzzlement:

- YOU DO read that in the paper, don't you? Well, I think it MUST happen to THEM. Well, they couldn't imagine it, surely? I mean, when they say things move and all THAT. They do, don't they?
  [G. B.: Well, I don't know, it's never happened to me.] No, nor to me either. If they get a minister to come and exorcise it—? When I read about it, I've believed it. I don't think you can imagine things like that. I know people are queer, but— (Meg)

- Well! I don't know what to think! There must be something in it. Something must have happened. They can't possibly have imagined it, all the tremors and things, can they? I shouldn't think so, anyway. (Lettie)

Because eventually their "proofs" stand or fall by whether these sources can be relied upon, believers are intensely aware of their opponents' case. So they insist that their informants are of the *highest* probity, the perception seen or remembered with *the most distinct* clarity, and, moreover, that such cases are both numerous and well-documented and *do not depend on the evidence of a single person*, however reliable.

- The people who've reported these things are people that you can rely on their word about it. I mean— you get ministers of the Church of England, who SWEAR that they've heard this sort of thing. (Dora).

- It wasn't that she'd been drinking. She was very SOBER! (Alma)

- This man was in the 8th Army. He wasn't FRIGHTENED or anything. (Winifred)

I would suggest that the sharing of experience—and, subsequently, the defence of the chosen interpretation—creates and maintains a "grammar of discourse" on the unofficial level. The supernatural is a topic that is debated frequently and seriously in informal situations, so that individuals are pressurized into taking sides, and they adopt the discourse by learning from those on their side in the philosophical tug-of-war. Traditions of belief and disbelief are learned through folkloric processes such as face-to-face communication, the sharing of information, and the telling of stories; and the rhetoric and arguments of both traditions are familiar and available to all. In my own fieldwork I found that primarily "rationalist" people were able to recite the arguments for the opposing supernaturalist tradition perfectly well. They could counter them in their own discourse, and did, on occasion, even use these arguments themselves. The same applied to those with primarily "supernaturalist" orientations.

It is my own belief that rationalism and supernaturalism are cultural options, competing discourses; and that neither is "better" or less "superstitious" than the other.

Though this book will recognize both traditions, its primary focus will be on the "traditions of belief," because they are so generally neglected in elite, popular, and folkloric discourses. The next chapter, in particular, will focus on believers' opinions and stories as they struggle to find interpretations of their experiences.

Chapter 2
Contact with the Dead

IN THIS CHAPTER, I TURN FROM AN EXAMINATION OF THE COMPETING cultures of belief and disbelief to focus primarily on the believers' discourse. I want to discuss three related concepts—life after death, visitations, and ghosts—as represented in the memorates the Manchester women shared with me.

Memorates are very good guides to living traditions. They are less influenced by the stereotypes of literature and popular culture than legends and more likely to reflect concepts current in the narrator's home community. Through them, we can see not only how culture shapes individual experience, but also how individuals shape the cultural traditions of their social group. None of these stories was requested. They were spontaneously volunteered, most of them as responses to questions of faith. They were offered because the speaker thought they were helpful illustrations of her point of view. So this chapter will be full of stories. It will also contain discussions of the stories via techniques which highlight many of their underlying themes and assumptions: that is, word lists and the analysis of recurring patterns.[1]

LIFE AFTER DEATH

Any discussion about the interaction of the dead and the living must be seen in the context of popular religion and ideas about life after death. I often used a composite question to initiate conversation on this subject: "Do you think that we might meet the dead again in another world, or is it possible that they might return in this one as some people seem to think?" Most people ignored the first part of the question and homed in on the second, but there were enough replies to at least get a feel for their approach to the larger metaphysical question.

The positive answers followed a consistent pattern: all were based on the premise that life would be futile unless it had some purpose or some chance of continuing in another sphere. The women said, "It would be very disappointing to go through life and not have a feeling that there's something there." After that, their answers took the form of looking for scriptural evidence or puzzling out the form such an afterlife might take.

A few women were sadly preoccupied with wrongs they had done to those now gone, or with failed relationships now beyond repair, but most were comforted by the thought of meeting dead loved ones in some form or other after death. Though they were often careful to speak of "SOULS rising again" or of contact with the dead being "only a SPIRITUAL thing," their faith in an afterlife was at heart a surprisingly material one. If the souls of the dead survive with the personality intact, as they seemed to believe, it is logical to think that memory and affection also remain. It also follows that these spirits must *be* somewhere, and not necessarily far away. Abigail and Mary expressed the prevailing ideas most aptly:

- Well, it's Saint Paul, wasn't it, said, "We're encompassed with a great cloud of witnesses." So I do think that they have some interest in the people left behind. (Abigail)

- I think they're here. I don't believe that there's a deadline, and, above, that's heaven, and below, that's earth underneath it. I don't believe that.
  [G. B.: They have to be around us somewhere?]
  Yes! That's why you suddenly sense a presence, isn't it? (Mary)

Though only a third of the women gave direct answers to questions about life after death, the majority of those said they believed in an afterlife, and it is impossible to understand their answers to the second part of the question except in this context. It is also in the context of this view that women said "the dead never leave me" and expected to be understood at both the metaphorical and the literal level. Alternatively, they spoke of their attachment to their homes or to photographs of dead friends thus:

- I've been there forty-five years. I wouldn't really like to leave there, because I always feel that my mother and father are there. (Catherine)

- I don't take flowers to the cemetery at anniversaries. I put them in the house, near the picture, and I say, "This is where they are. They're with me." (Kate)

These sorts of formulation also give a clue to the way the women see the spiritual world entering the mundane one—that is, through people and places. As I have said, I was concerned during my fieldwork to follow up clues which the women themselves let fall and to adapt my vocabulary and concepts to the ones they were familiar with. The result was the discovery of their taxonomy of the supernatural world: on the one hand, there are the loving souls of good people who come to those who loved them in life and continue to provide protection and reassurance; on the other hand, there are "THINGS in houses," evil spirits of the restless dead who haunt the places where they have died unnaturally or committed wicked deeds.

The women may have perhaps believed in other types of encounters as well but, if they did, they never mentioned it. No one invoked legendary motifs such as haunted gardens, churchyards, and crossroads, or relied on traditional stereotypes such as animal ghosts (though one story does feature the ghost of a beloved cat). It may be that these were not part of their world view—or maybe they were not mentioned simply because the subject never came up in conversation: it is hard to tell. It is possible, therefore, that the picture painted here is partial and incomplete, but what we *have* got is a clear and full description of two opposed poles of belief—place-centered evil and purposeless manifestations on the one hand, and the people-centered and purposeful visitations on the other.

It is perhaps surprising to find that almost half of those asked believed in hauntings or, as they often termed it, "THINGS in houses." Though the women I spoke to were more reluctant to talk about ghosts than any other topic—less inclined to tell stories or expand their answers beyond a brief "yes" or "no" (there were only forty-seven direct answers to this question and only seven stories)—they obviously do still think there may be something in these beliefs, and their concepts fit remarkably well into a familiar pattern of mysterious footsteps, self-flushing toilets, cold winds from nowhere, displaced objects, lights, and rappings (compare Jones 1959).

These occurrences are thought to be caused by "suicides and murders and things like that," or perhaps—alarmingly—by "evil spirits." The story below told by Joan, a married woman in her seventies, while not indicating any real belief in ghosts, does show what sorts of things are supposed to happen when "evil spirits" are about:[2]

- Ha hmmh! This makes me laugh! I was doing some sewing, Ooh it's about a month ago now, and I have an electric sewing machine and I can't thread this sewing machine without— one of Singer's—
  [G. B.: those little things they have—]
  . . . to put it through. Well! during the course of the afternoon that disappeared, and also a red flannel—tab-thing I keep needles in, that disappeared too, and I've never been able to find either of them since! and yet! they were never taken out of the room as far as I know and I said to myself, "I wonder if there's any evil spirits lurking about?"

The same assumption about the sorts of things ghosts are likely to do lies behind a sixty-year-old dressmaker's account of her terror at finding her cutting-out shears and bobbins arranged in a neat pattern on the hall carpet.

Elsewhere, speakers give accounts of hearing mysterious footsteps or other noises, of seeing windows or doors shut of their own accord, of strange feelings, of breezes, and apparitions of unknown people:

- I met one lady and she said the house was kind of haunted. They heard things going on and that. Anyway they left it in the end. But funny things used to happen when they lived there. (Clara)

- Again, I remember Wolfgang, a German boy who used to stay with us, telling us the story about his uncle, the pastor. He had an uncle who was a Lutheran pastor, and the uncle told him or it was strong family knowledge.

  They moved into this equivalent to the Manse, whatever they call it, and it was quite empty and not a very nice sort of place altogether. It was a bit grim, and his uncle wasn't a bit happy about it.

  But, anyway, they settled down, the family did, and he was in his study writing his sermons, and suddenly all his books came off the shelf and flew all over the place, and his papers, his sermons, were all fluttering about like leaves, and the uncle wasn't really very concerned, he thought there was a sudden wind though there wasn't a window open or anything, and he went out into the other room, passage, or what-have-you, and asked his wife and she said, "No. Nothing. Why? What do you mean?" and it happened again. Every time he went to sit down to do any study, all his papers flew up all over the place.

  Now, I know to make the story REAL, I should say what it was that had CAUSED this, and Wolfgang did connect it up to something, but that I've forgotten. (Agnes)

- Well, I think there's something must be there, but what it is I don't know. But there must be something for the church to—
  [G. B.: Well, they have services for it, don't they?]

Yes. Yes. I was told about this when we lived in Bangor. My father, this is going back a good few years, he used to do a lot of reading.

This was before television and I think he must have been reading. My mother was in bed, and all of a sudden he came BOUNDING up the stairs! He said he'd been SAT there and all of a sudden he heard footsteps coming up the cellar stairs!

He wasn't imagining it, and he was so scared my MOTHER had to go DOWN!

But there was nobody there. What it was, I don't know, but I don't think he was imagining it whatever it was. (Lydia)

The structure of these narratives is suggestive of their psychology. All deal with the inherent threat of the unexplained. They describe natural occurrences that have no discernible natural causation. So a cause is sought in unhappy or violent past events:[3] as Agnes says, "to make the story REAL, I should say what it was that had CAUSED this." Even if, as in Clara's story, no past events are uncovered that would explain the things that are "going on" in the house, a cause—a supernatural cause—is implied, for the family to have to leave.

A lexical analysis shows that the words which crop up most frequently in stories about hauntings are, apart from the word "house" itself, "go," "attic," "stairs," "door," "somebody," "cellar," "nightmare," "family," and "disappear." Haunted places are thus seen to be no-go areas such as cellars and attics, or betwixt-and-between places such as stairs and doorways; the experience is nightmarish, the ghost is a stranger, a "somebody" who disappears, and the family has to leave everything and "go." All these expressions and assumptions may be found time and time again in accounts of hauntings from medieval sermon stories to popular ghost gazetteers.

One explanation for this consistency might be that these actually are the typical contexts for paranormal experiences (though why this should be so is a question that needs to be answered). Alternatively, this interpretation might be reversed by saying that these sorts of locations, being the stuff of thousands of

"Alas, Poor Ghost!"

ghost stories, will predispose susceptible people to see ghosts there. Perception psychologists might take this view, and many folklorists might agree (see, for example, Honko 1964). Other folklorists might prefer to interpret it as the shaping of private experience into public narrative. They would suggest that telling other people about strange happenings is a way of dealing with them and the more people narrate to each other, the more their stories become traditionalized. So, personal experience gradually acquires the traditional trappings of darkness, solitude, and liminality, and begins to resemble a conventional ghost story.

One can see these processes at work very clearly in a sad, strange little story which Inez, a widow in her seventies, tells. She is presented with a very peculiar domestic situation for which no rules of interpretation exist. She can only explain the situation to herself in terms of conventional ghostlore, and yet she knows that it is neither quite appropriate nor relevant to her situation:

- Now, this is a funny thing. I married a man who had been married before, and when we came to set up our own house he had everything from the old house brought in and it had to be exactly in the same way. Nothing had to be altered, and if any china was broken, it had to be bought just the same. I didn't realize this, mind you, when I married him, but still—

  There was a big photograph of his wife— a big lithograph, really, of his wife, right over the mantelpiece, sitting in a chair, and I used to have nightmares she wasn't really dead. She was alive in the attic. We hadn't GOT an attic! Or she was in the basement room, which we hadn't got either, neither attic or basement!

  But I had to do everything in the house as she said so, and when I went cleaning round the house, sometimes I'd knock myself against the sideboard or whatever, and I'd feel she'd knocked me against the sideboard. This was just because I had to have everything the same, you know, that's the only thing.

  But to think she was alive and telling me— and that if I got knocked or trapped in the furniture, I thought she was doing it. It did affect me, as I say, always having this photograph in front of me, and having to have everything the same way.

For about a fortnight before the anniversary of her death he wouldn't speak to you. He was always rushing off, you know to the cemetery. Of all the days in the year, Christmas Day it was too! You kind of felt she was the boss, you know.

Alongside accounts of full-blown hauntings and unclassifiable experiences such as Inez's, there are also vague and unspecific references to "happy" and "unhappy" houses:

- A happy house. Sometimes if you go into a house you think, "Oh I feel happy here" and other houses, "No, I'm not very keen on that house." (Audrey)

- If you go into a house you know what it feels like. You feel the atmosphere when you walk in. (Mary)

- Most houses I've been in have been very friendly. (Patricia)

- But the people have all been good who've been in that house. My sister said she felt happy whenever she came into it. She's been so happy since she went in there. (Vera)

- There's one or two places that I hate and always have, and I don't know why. I think there are places that emanate sort of malignant, sort of nasty feelings. (Agnes)

These accounts, while perhaps reflecting a tradition less influenced by literature and popular stereotypes than full-blown hauntings, yet help further unravel the rationale behind them and show both concepts as aspects of a single idea. Words like "atmosphere" and "feelings" keep recurring. So do references to unhappiness, suicides, "wrongness," and divorce; or, alternatively, happiness, goodness, and loveliness. Here is a story told by a younger married woman, Berenice*:[4]

- I'm in two schools of thought about that.

  Because I can go into— I've gone into a really grotty property and thought, "Oh, this is lovely!" I've gone into a beautiful new house or bungalow and said, "Oh, I couldn't live here!" The house, there's an ATMOSPHERE, something WRONG with it, I can't put my finger on it.

  But a friend of ours (funny little story, I don't know whether it will interest you) but he moved from Priestley after he got married, remarried, wanted to move out of the area, so he went to live at Colmworth, and he [had been] in this house for quite a while very happily, [then] decided that one across the town— was a bit bigger and rather liked it, and they moved into it.

  They actually moved into this house, and they got everything straight, and he sat down with a cup of coffee and a cigarette, and he says, "I can't stay here. We're moving out!" and he hadn't even SLEPT in the house, and his wife played POP with him!

  Now, he is a very sensitive man, for a man particularly sensitive, and they renegotiated and they bought their old house back.

  But, I mean, everybody laughed at him.

  But there must have been something in it because— [laughs].

When the women discuss the matter in more detail, a clear and consistent picture emerges. As they see it, the events and emotions of former residents' lives remain locked in the form of "energy" or "waves" or an "aura" in the house where they lived. If it is pleasant, the present resident can absorb and benefit from the atmosphere; the memories in the house will make those who live in it happy, healthy, and wise. If the spirit is malignant, however, and the memories violent, the energy may transform itself into a force which can throw or displace objects or echo the events of real life by sighing, walking about, switching lights on or off, closing doors, flushing toilets, and so on. Alternatively, it may simply create an atmosphere so unpleasant that it cannot be endured. This is, both literally and metaphorically, the "spirit" of the house. "We lived in a house that was spirited," Molly* told me:

- It was a lady committed suicide in the house, and then no one would live in it. We lived in it. We were desperate for another house. We went to live in it.

  We had all kinds of things happened. Otherwise I wouldn't have believed in it, because I do believe in spirits. I don't say ghosts. I don't know whether they're the same. I imagine they are really.

  [G. B.: What happened there?]

  Oh, well, the toilet used to flush when nobody was in, and we'd hear somebody walking in the passage and we'd go to the door and there'd be nobody there, and my mother was hanging washing up one day in the attic (you know, we'd two big attics) and she was hanging washing up one day and somebody came up behind her and gripped her by the shoulders, and she thought it was one of us, but it wasn't.

  We didn't live long in that house. It got a bit unnerving.

The older the house, the more likely it is to have a history which may thus manifest itself. Agnes, a married woman in her sixties, puts this well when she said:

- If it is possible you can get the voices of people who are living, you can get their voices in the air, that people can speak to you on the telephone from Australia, New Zealand, as if they were in the same room; and I've read or heard that every single word that's ever been spoken, every sound that's ever been made since the world came into being, is still here. Well, I think that your vibrations are all around you, and if there's evil, Hitler, or

"Alas, Poor Ghost!"

any of the dreadful atrocities, burnings at the stake, there's been heaps and heaps through history. You couldn't have terror and horror and violent physical pain and hatred and evil and it just disappears, just because the people have died. It's still there! And the same with very good people.

This logical reasoning makes the foundation of the believers' case. In addition, they are able to point to the existence of the ceremony of exorcism, to the many reports of "reliable people," and to the unlikelihood of several people spontaneously "imagining" identical phenomena in a single location or of people wanting to deceive others on such an important point.

Popular science, oral tradition, peer-group discussion, literary ghost stories, films, and TV, therefore, all combine to provide a coherent tradition with an appealing rationale—a lively tradition of the restless dead.

VISITATIONS

At the other end of the spectrum are the good dead whose presence is felt, or who are heard or glimpsed around the house by those who loved them in life. Whereas the ghosts which haunt houses are unknown and unwelcome intruders, these are visitations from loved and familiar people—trusted, needed, and welcomed. In life they were figures of power and authority (husbands and mothers), close siblings, or deeply loved children, or members of the caring outer circle of the family (aunts and uncles, nieces and nephews, grandparents). This community of the loving dead is thought to surround living people and may occasionally interact with them, effortlessly bridging the gap between the spiritual and the mundane worlds.

The Manchester women were far happier to talk about these sorts of experiences (sixty-seven out of the eighty-seven women answered my questions on this topic and told more than seventy stories). Unlike the purposeless manifestations in "wrong" or "nasty" houses, visitations from the good dead are never dressed up in the familiar paraphernalia of legendary hauntings. Indeed, word lists drawn from these stories confound many popular expectations. They show that, whereas stories of ghosts and "WRONG houses" are couched in terms of conventional "spookiness"—attics, cellars, stairs, doors, nightmares, a mysterious "somebody" who haunts the house and "disappears"—the good dead are described in subjective terms and reflect family relationships ("feel," "see," "think," "say," "come," "(a)live," "there," "mother," and "father" are the most frequently recurring words used). Their presence is seen as an extension of ordinary family life. Dead loved ones are thought to exist alongside the living rather than to have returned from a distinctly separate place, as the relational prepositions the women use in their stories show ("to," "with," "by," "beside," "around," and "in," which all imply nearness, are used five times more frequently than words like "back" and "from"). Another interesting thing to note is that, though the word "feel" occurs most frequently in the stories, the word "see" is the next most frequent; and that the women explicitly say that they "plainly" saw the dead person more often than they use vague, face-saving formulations such as "it was as though he was there" (see appendix 5).

One essential difference between evil and good manifestations is always the absence or presence of *purpose*. Evil occurrences are meaningless and intrusive disturbances of the natural order. Benevolent manifestations, on the other hand, are not only caused by events in the mundane world, but are also purposefully directed towards them. Whereas ghosts have "no business to be here" in both senses of the phrase, visitants have every reason to be around. They are recalled to the realm of the living by events occurring there. They not only have a reason for appearing, but often a role to play.

This contrast is very neatly demonstrated in a little memorate about a lost playing card:

- And then one night (NOW, this is the thing that made me believe it!), I'm very fond of playing patience. It's a form of therapy when I'm depressed, I play patience, and Johnny, that was my late husband, always used to steal up behind me and pinch a card, and I was playing patience one day, and I got the first lot out: they were

"Alas, Poor Ghost!"

all there the first game. The second game, I found out the two of spades was missing.

Now I only play patience in the lounge. I never play it in the dining room. So, I searched high and low for this two of spades, and I could not find it anywhere. I looked under the cushions, you know how you look anywhere for things? And then, about three days after, the rent man came, and I always take him into the dining room to pay the rent, and I hadn't been in the dining room because I only use the dining room in the summer, there's no heating in it except the electric fire, and DO YOU KNOW that in the center of the table was that two of spades? DEAD CENTER.

So, of course, I went to Miss Luke [the medium]. It did quite frighten me. It STARTLED ME. "Oh," she said, "that was Johnny playing one of his tricks on you!"

Wasn't THAT strange? (Audrey)

Audrey is alarmed when she finds that an object (the playing card) has been displaced, for it is just this kind of causeless and meaningless activity that is associated with haunted houses. The occurrence quite literally does not make *sense*: "It did quite frighten me. It STARTLED ME," says Audrey. The medium, however, allays her fears by reinterpreting the experience for her, and she does this by introducing the idea that the removal of the card was deliberate—one of the late Johnny's practical jokes. From being a meaningless and disorderly happening, it becomes proof of the continued presence of the loving, if mischievous, Johnny: the "thing that made" Audrey "believe it," as she says. This radical reinterpretation has been achieved simply by introducing the idea of purposefulness.

CAUSE, CONSEQUENCE, AND LACK LIQUIDATED

Notions of cause and consequence, purpose and order, run through all the stories the women tell about the good dead. They are so basic to belief, so entrenched in traditional habits of thought, that they structure the narratives themselves. By following these clues we are able to distinguish aspects of the women's beliefs about the influence of the spiritual world on the earthly sphere.

When telling stories about visitations, the women commonly select from five standard components. As well as the opening and closing remarks which mark the borderline between narrative and ordinary conversation (called here the story "aperture" and "closure"), there are three central elements. There is a scene-setting which often analyzes the state of mind or health of the protagonist as well as setting the physical scene; a description of the event itself; and a resolution, the "what happened next" story element which announces the consequence of the events. A good deal of useful information may be obtained by looking at which of these elements are used in the story and how they are arranged.

Cause

One group of narratives uses the first two of the core elements to outline the circumstances and the event. The narrator often takes a good deal of trouble to describe the precise conditions, stressing dates and times and places, or giving the history of a fatal or near-fatal illness, or otherwise establishing beyond doubt that there was good reason for the visitation which she then goes on to tell of. The following accounts are typical:

- But I saw my father.

     My father was the first to die, and he died at three o'clock in the morning, and then twelve months after, Mother died at three o'clock in the afternoon. Well, she died from cancer of the jaw, so I mean, there was nothing to SMILE about.

     But just before she died, I felt that whatever there was, EVER there was, Father had come to meet her.

     Because she just sat up and she gave that SMILE.

     Of course, I think they do sit up before they die.

     But— and she sort of held her arms out, and it was just that SPECIAL SMILE she always kept for him—
     [G. B.: You think she actually saw him?]
     I do! Oh, yes! (Lettie)

- But I do think you can see people that's died.

  I do think there's summat at the other side and I've experienced it, as I say, and my daughter (she lives in Corbridge now, her youngest daughter's nearly sixteen now) and when she was only about three it was the kidneys that were wrong with her, and they sent a district nurse to her.

  My daughter had a very bad time with that last child. She's four of them, two married now, one [other?] still at home. And she was very close to her father, my daughter was, she was the oldest, and I didn't know for quite a long while after (and I knew it must have been the crisis, my granddaughter must have been passing through the crisis, because she seemed to turn after that, on the mend), and I didn't know for quite a long while after, and my daughter said, "Mum," she said, "I've SEEN MY DAD as plain as I can see you! and he STOOD at the bottom of the bed as though she was going to die."

  She says, "He was ready to take her!" But she turned for the better, you see.

  But she said, "He STOOD at the bottom of that bed with his arms up!"

  Some people think you imagine these things, but no! I'VE HEARD MY HUSBAND'S VOICE, and there's not been a soul in that flat! (Kathleen)

These themes are frequently echoed in non-narrative remarks like: "I've heard people say that just before you die, you seem to SEE them," or "I only believe they might come back at your death." They are also the ideas which structure an account of a recent illness:

- But I'll tell you something. I haven't even told my sister this.

  I've been quite ill just recently, and it's been one of those horrible things that didn't get diagnosed until it was almost too late. I hadn't been feeling well for well over a year, and I'd put on an awful lot of weight and was so tired that it was like an illness. I just couldn't drag myself around. I don't know how I dragged myself around, and fortunately for me, I got two lumps in my neck, and, of course, this started the ball rolling then. They were thyroids, I had an inactive thyroid.

But I just couldn't go to the office or anything like that at all. It was just impossible, and I was so tired and so weary, when I dozed off in a chair it wasn't like an ordinary little catnap, it was almost like a coma, and there was so many times during that short period WHEN I USED TO IMAGINE my mother was coming into the room, and she'd been dead for about fifteen or sixteen years. Nineteen sixty-four, seventeen years at the end of the year.

[G. B.: You never actually saw her?]

No, it was just a feeling. I haven't even told my sister, and I felt at times almost as if she was talking to me, and I just passed it up because I don't really believe it. (Clara)

When I remark, "That's where you differ from a lot of people, because a lot of people would say she was really there—," Clara replies, "Well, if I had thought that, I'd have been really sure I was dying, because I would have thought, 'Oh, my GOD! This seeing my mother's DYING!' But I don't think that way at all."[5] She thereby expresses belief even as she denies it, and illustrates its nature even as she dismisses it.

Another story of this "cause" type does not feature any sort of physical manifestation, but was contributed during a discussion about the return of the dead. It shows, I think, that it is commonly thought that the death of someone close is often accompanied by some sort of unusual experience—here, a telepathic communication between a dying woman and her sister:

- My sister died some years ago and she was desperately ill, and we'd been to see her in hospital the Sunday, and on the Sunday evening, the specialist phoned and said that the crisis was over and she would be on the mend, and I could HEAR her TALKING to me ALL evening, and suddenly, at five to six she just said, "I'm sorry, Sylvia, I can't hold on any longer," and the phone went, and it was the hospital. She'd died at five to six.

But it was as if she was actually in the room with me and said, "I'm sorry, Sylvia, I can't hold on any more." (Sylvia*)

Four more stories do not actually feature visitations, but are more akin to the so-called "near death experience" (Atwater 1988; Greyson and Flynn 1984; Holck 1978–79; Moody 1975; Ring 1980; Ring and Franklin 1981–82; Thomas, Cooper, and Suscovich 1982–83; see also Basford 1990). They do, however, provide additional evidence that it is commonly thought that the dying are afforded some kind of supernatural experience and that these visions, being glimpses of the next world, are signs of impending death. In one such story a dying person sees "the Master," and in another a fatally sick man keeps saying, "What a beautiful picture!" In a third, the narrator tells how her husband died exclaiming, "It's wonderful! It's wonderful." In a fourth, a dying grandfather sees the gates of heaven:

- When my grandfather was dying, and my grandmother's name was Kate, and I was with him when he died, and he said— he called me Kate for about a day before he died and he said, "I'd like this, Kate"— and as he was dying he suddenly grasped my hand and he said, "Oh, smell the flowers! Smell the lilacs!" and he said, "Open the gate, Kate! I can't get in!" and it was February, there were no flowers out and none in his room, and he said it so strongly, "Smell the lilacs! Smell the lilacs!" and "Open the gate, Kate. I can't get in!" (Margot)

What is in common between all these accounts is the emphasis the storytellers place on the *context* of the occurrence. In every case, careful attention is given to dates and times and persons. Lettie, for example, is exact about both the father's and the mother's deaths, matching them up neatly; Kathleen gives a mini-history of her daughter's life and relationship with her late father; and Clara is specific about the onset of her illness, its duration, and the period that has elapsed since her mother's death. The obvious implication is that the extraordinary conditions explain the extraordinary events and thus authenticate them. Throughout, there runs a theme of order and purpose.

Consequence

In another group of narratives the "cause" element is absent or minimal, and the narrator focuses on the remaining elements, the visitation and its outcome. There seem to be no precipitating conditions which can account for the visitation—no sickness, no danger, no dying. Into this ordinary environment steps the extraordinary in the shape of some loved person known to be a long way away. He or she is, of course, dead or dying in that far place, and has come to say farewell.

A story (told by Ella, a married woman in her seventies) may serve as illustration of this type of narrative because of its typical contents:

- My husband during the war well, it was during the First World War really. Well, at the end. He was young. He was at home. But he was away with his sister and they—

  The young man his sister was engaged to, because she was a bit older than he was, he appeared before them in the bedroom as plain as anything in his uniform. He said it was just as if he was almost there, and he'd been killed just at that time in the war.

  Sixteen or seventeen he [the husband] was. But he said he [the brother-in-law] was standing near the dressing table and you just— he could have sworn he was there, and he apparently had been killed about that time in France or something, and that was something—

  He'd experienced it. There's no doubt.

In Ella's story the scene is briefly set in such a way that we can see there was nothing in the percipient's life that would precipitate a visitation. She then moves straight on to describing how the brother-in-law's wraith appeared to them, and ends with the information that explains the experience, "and he'd been killed just at that time in the war." As so many memorate-tellers do (see chapter 4), she then begins again, adds a bit of extra information, then winds the story up with an evaluative gloss as a "closure."

In other "consequence" stories, trouble of some kind is the result, not the cause, of the visitation. This may be a burglary, an illness, or an accident, as in two little illustrative stories told by Dora, a single woman in her seventies, and Carrie, a widow of the same age. Dora's story, the first of those below, is constructed on a consequence-happening-consequence pattern; Carrie's on an even more circular pattern composed entirely of a cycle of consequence-happening elements.

- They had burglars in the house about two years ago [*consequence*], and, just before this happened, one of my aunts APPEARED to her (my aunt died four years ago), and she actually SAW her but she didn't SAY anything [*event*].

    She said to me afterwards, "I'm sure she was trying to WARN me" [*consequence*].

- Well, it's FUNNY. DO YOU KNOW, if anyone's going to be ill in my family [*consequence*], my mother comes TO me. I always know. My mother comes TO me [*event*].

    You know, when our Wilfred used to be ill, I used to get on the phone and I'd say, "Hello, Florrie. How are you?" and she'd say, "I'm all right. But WILFRED'S in bed" [*consequence*] and before I had my back done, like before I fell in the cemetery [*consequence*], in the night my mother come to me and she says, "You can't SLEEP," or something like that, "You can't SLEEP, can you?" She's STOOD at the side of the bed [*event*], and I've not been well since [*consequence*].

    Isn't it STRANGE how she comes TO me every time? [*event*].
    [G. B.: You can actually see her?]

YES. She's stood at the side of the bed, and then it's gone [*event*].

Usually the visitation which heralds a death is of a known member of the family. So here, in the second type of story told by the Manchester women, visitations are revealed in a thoroughly traditional light as omens of death and danger. A basic assumption which structures these stories is the expectation that visitations from dead friends and family are purposeful, and that there is a message of some kind to be conveyed. When no cause can be seen for the visitation in the present, then it is assumed that the message must relate to the future. It is reasoned that the dead person must know something the survivors don't and has come to alert them to the danger.

Lack Liquidated

Other narratives have a neatly symmetrical structure. They consist of an account of the cause of the occurrence in terms of the context or the condition of the percipient; a description of the encounter itself; and a résumé of its consequences—with the first and last of these elements predominating and matched together. The cause of the visitation is invariably shown to be some sort of "lack" in the narrator's life and the consequence is invariably seen to be the "liquidation" of that lack (Propp 1968, 35, 53). The "lack" can be in any area of daily life: it may be a lack of mental or physical health; a lack of knowledge or vital information in domestic arrangements, finance, business, or working life; or any sort of danger or distress. This critical "lack" is "liquidated" by the dead lending a hand—the sick are returned to health, the lost object is found, necessary advice is received, and so on.

This pattern, and the logic that underlies it, can be seen very simply by taking a selection of stories and comparing the "cause" and the "consequence" elements of the story as below:

- [*Cause (lack)*] . . . and she was very ill. She'd measles very badly and was in a bad way actually.
  [*Consequence (lack liquidated)*]But from then on, funnily enough she was all right. She improved. (Ella)

- [*Cause (lack)*] I went through quite a bad time a few years ago.
  [*Consequence (lack liquidated)*] I got help. (Violet)

- [*Cause (lack)*] . . . and the horse, the leading horse (he had two on this occasion) slipped and fell, and he didn't know what to do a little bit.
  [*Consequence (lack liquidated)*] . . . and the leading horse got up and he was able to go, and he got to Bradbury very shaken, very frightened, but his load intact. (Agnes)

- [*Cause (lack)*] So he said, "I don't know where the damn thing is."
  [*Consequence (lack liquidated)*] So I pulled the paper up and there it was. (Maura)

Women tell how the dead have intervened in times of sickness, how they have helped them make successful house sales or find lost document, how they have given them timely instructions, or strength and skill at moments of crisis. These events always happen in familiar surroundings—the bedroom principally, but also elsewhere in the house. Only in Agnes's story do events happen away from the home. Mothers are the most common type of visitant, then fathers and husbands. Children and friends figure in four stories and a brother, a grandmother, and a "lady in white" in three more. The "lady in white" is the sole example of an unknown and unnamed visitant.[6] In half the cases, the stories involve some sort of communication between the dead and the living: words like "tell" and "say" recur very frequently. On some of these occasions the visitant's voice is plainly heard but just as frequently the communication is a telepathic one. In five stories the narrator actually sees her visitor and in another five she "feels her presence." As many women insist that they heard or saw the dead person "quite clearly" as say that "it was only a spiritual thing" or it was "as though" he or she was really there. Similarly, fairly equal numbers of women tell, on the one hand, of events which happened once or twice on specific, well-remembered occasions; and, on the other hand, of "feelings" that are "always with" them in whatever they are doing. Four typical stories, arranged on a continuum from least to most explicit, show the uniformity of the theme but the contrasts in the way it is presented:

- My mother's been dead a long time, but I always feel that if I'm in any trouble, I can feel the nearness of my mother. I mean, my mother was a good woman, we were all brought up Chapel, and I feel as though she's near me and she helps me. It doesn't make it any easier for me. I mean, it doesn't go away. But I feel she's there.

  I went through a very bad time quite a few years ago. My husband had a very bad illness. I couldn't have gone through that on my own strength.

  Now, whether that help came from up above, which I really think it did, I got help, and my mother was at the side of me I'M SURE! Because I couldn't have gone through it on my own. I lost four of my family in three months.

  So, as I say, I DIDN'T BEAR THAT ON MY OWN. I did come through it, and I really do think— I always feel that in any time of trouble my mother, not my father, my mother is very close by me. (Violet)[7]

- [G. B.: Did you ever have anything like this happen?]
  Only when I was doing that house, and yet I wasn't a bit afraid of it!
  [Rachel's daughter (aside): Bill, that was her brother who'd died, told her how to paint the house for his wife to sell.]
  [G. B.: What about that? What Bill told you?]
  Well, like, when I was doing the cupboard, he'd say, "Now tosh inside that corner, Rachel!"
  [G. B.: Tosh?]
  Paint. That's a right old-fashioned word for "paint." "Now tosh inside that corner, Rachel. Do it proper." AND YET! I didn't turn round to look for him, but it was his voice, and he HELPED me to paint that house! It's

really funny. He said, "Paint it lightly and very quickly. Paint it light and very quick, the gloss paint, not like the other, the undercoat—," and honestly, he helped me paint that house!

Well, I think he wanted to thwart my brother-in-law, because he was right nasty about it. He said, "You won't get a b- hundred pounds for that house!" and we got £390 for our Ellie, Bill's widow like. That's a long while since, love, and I went up every night, four doors away, and I painted the lot! Kitchen and all! I did! Upstairs! Everywhere! and it looked something like when I'd finished, you know, and I was really proud of it!

But prouder when the money came and our Ellie had her share, and I never told my husband. He used to say, "There's a terrible smell of paint, Rachel," and I said, "Get away! You've got paint on the nerves, Arthur!" But he must have been right, because it was me, you know! I'd a pair of our Bill's old overalls and I used to put them on when I went up, and I FELT HE WAS HELPING ME. It's true! and I could have stopped there all night, and Arthur says, "Where the hell have you been?" and I said, "I've been right over the back with the dog."

Poor Judy! Poor Judy had never been anywhere! If only that dog could have talked, she'd have had a story to tell! (Rachel)

• Dad had been dead now for about three years probably. Ned was working at the time of the story for a local farmer, Sam Black at the Manor Farm at Dell, and he used to have to go to market with these cart horses, bigger horses than ours but still cart horses, and he was going to Bradbury market one terrible frosty day. It was a dark morning, early morning, and the leading horse slipped and fell.

Ned would be at this time only fifteen or sixteen at the most and no experience. He was stuck in a country lane with a horse and the load all UP like this. The one horse had dragged the other horse down, and he didn't know what to do a little bit! and he said (this is the story), you know how you do? "Oh, help me! help me! What shall I do? What shall I do?" and saying it out loud, and he said Dad's voice CAME TO HIM QUITE CLEARLY, said, "Cut the girth cord, Ned! Cut the girth cord!" and he cut the girth cord and the leading horse got up and he was able to go, and he got to Bradbury very shaken, very frightened, but the load intact. (Agnes)

- But I know— a cousin of mine, she was very, very old when she died. She was very sensitive. We knew her mother wouldn't last, she was downstairs.

  My cousin had gone to bed. They'd been sitting up with the mother, and she had gone to bed, and she said her father came and woke her and he said, "Your mother wants you," and she got up, went downstairs, and her brother was there and he said, "What have you come for?" and she said, "Well, my father came and said she needed me."

  He said, "Father? Father's dead!" and she said,— it was only after— She said, "Oh," she said, "He came in. I heard him cough, and he came in," and he shook her and said, "Your mother wants you," and she got up, and she said it was only when her brother said, "Father? Father's dead!" AND HE'D BEEN DEAD YEARS.
  [G. B.: What happened next?]
  Oh, she died. She died very soon after that. (Alma)

Such beliefs in the power of the dead to see and intervene in the affairs of ordinary life have power to explain a wide range of strange occurrences, for example, that commonplace, but yet perplexing, experience of the surfacing of unconscious into conscious thought—those familiar, involuntary perceptions, intuitions, and recurrent thoughts that seemingly miraculously solve long-standing problems. One informant, Maura, a widow in her seventies, for example, has a long, complex account on this theme. She is asked by a friend to help him sort out the possessions of his late wife. During the clearing out, they find a letter from a building society

"Alas, Poor Ghost!"

about a substantial secret investment the wife had made. The widower cannot claim the money unless he can find the paying-in book, which, of course, he knows nothing about. Maura promptly says, without knowing why, "I expect it's hidden under the paper in the bottom of the wardrobe." And that is exactly where they find it. Maura interprets her sudden inspiration as a message from the dead woman. Similarly, in one of her many racy stories, Audrey tells how she loses her pension book:

- Well, it's a funny thing happened. I lost my pension book one day and I couldn't find this pension book anywhere. Now, I always put it in one place, keep it in one place. I have it in a pochette, you see. I'd taken my money out, I put my pension book back and I put it in the sideboard drawer which I've always done.

  So one Thursday, it was pension day, went to get it and it wasn't there! and I thought, "That's darned funny! I never left my pension book out at all!" and I searched and searched for it and couldn't find it anywhere, so I said, "It's no use! I'll have to go to the post office and see what the postmaster will say about this," and on my way to the post office something kept on saying in my brain, "Look behind the electric fire! LOOK BEHIND THE ELECTRIC FIRE!"

  Anyway, I went to the post office. I knew I hadn't lost it outside, and he said nobody had brought it in, and he said, "You'd better to go to the main post office," you see.

  So, coming back, this, LOOK BEHIND THE ELECTRIC FIRE, so I looked— when I got in— I looked behind the electric fire, and it was absolutely full of soot!

  Now, the lady upstairs, because I live in a downstairs flat, had had the chimney sweep in, and she'd said, "There's hardly any soot down my chimney," but it was all down mine!

  So I thought, "I'd better clean this out!" I did get lots of soot out!

  So, I cleaned this soot out and I thought, "Well, I'd better go down now and see about getting some money from the Social Security," and, as I was going out of the back door, I thought, "Those tissues look funny!" I keep some tissues on the Welsh dresser in the kitchen, and they were flat on there, you see, lying flat, you know. I thought, "Well! What's wrong with those tissues?" and I lifted the tissues up and underneath was my pension book!

Now I have an idea myself, I know it sounds silly, that Johnny wanted me to find out that there was soot behind the electric fire, because it was dangerous, you see, and I thought he thought the only way of telling me was to hide my pension book. It might just come into my head to say, "Look behind the electric fire." WASN'T THAT FUNNY?

Because, a pension book, I wouldn't dream of putting it underneath the tissues! I've always for years put it straight back as soon as I've taken the money out, so I know where it is.

But I think it was Johnny telling me. Don't you think that? (Audrey)

Whereas wraiths of the newly dead and dying, warning visitations, and so on are made meaningful by the interpretation put on them and not by virtue of anything they do, these sorts of visitations either directly or indirectly accomplish changes in the mundane world. In all these accounts, as in many others, the dead are shown as active for good—providing skill and information, carrying messages, reminding, strengthening, and supporting distressed survivors. They are part of a chain that reaches from the spiritual to the natural sphere. They therefore provide for the women the strongest possible evidence, not only of the survival of personal identity after death, but also of the continuance of the important structuring relationships of family and kinship: Heaven is all around and love defies death.

So it is that the women say:

- I'm not really religious, but I have beliefs. Since my husband died and I've been alone, there's such a lot of

"Alas, Poor Ghost!"

things that happen that I've thought, "Well, there must be somebody behind that's helping me." (Susan)

- I'm sure you must sometimes have said to yourself, "Oh, I wish I hadn't done that!" because something was telling you not to? What was that something? Perhaps it was from the spiritual world, I don't know. But something has told you NOT TO DO IT! (Julia)

Alternatively, they may refer to other people's experiences of such things and compare it to their own sad lack of such support:

- So many, I'm speaking of widows now, find comfort. They say, "My husband's walking beside me."
  "It must be a very good thing to have," I say. "What a help it must be! But," I've said, "I've tried. I've tried— not to CONTACT him but to feel he's around, but no. No!" (Dorothy)

- You do hear different people speak of it, that they've been in touch and all this sort of thing. But it's never happened to me. I can't say, "Well, yes, I had the feeling that a soul was at the side of me telling me anything." You know, you'll hear somebody say, "Well, I just sort of sensed that he was at the side of me." (Nadine)

- But you know they do say that if we pray hard enough for anyone ill or anything like that, the best will happen for them. How much more so, then, from someone who's transcended everything. (Ruth)

Thus it is the common opinion that the spiritual world permeates the mundane one. The dead are thus witnesses of the lives of those they have left behind, and may perpetuate their role of parent or spouse as mediators between two worlds, continuing to interest themselves in the small concerns of daily life and if necessary coming to the rescue, armed not only with their former love but also with their present superior knowledge. These are experiences the women spoke of extensively; but, though there is entrenched belief in the validity and reality of these sorts of experiences, and though it is obviously a traditional belief in the sense of being continuously and vigorously transmitted through an appropriate conduit (Dégh and Vázsonyi 1975), there is not even a name for such visitants. However, taking up Abigail's biblical reference—"It's Saint Paul, wasn't it, said, 'We're encompassed with a great cloud of witnesses.' So I do think that they have some interest in the people left behind"—I think of them as "witnesses."

This folklore of "witnesses" is a previously undocumented tradition, but it is possible to deduce from the stories women tell about them that witness experiences are thought to occur: either at night when one is in bed, the visitant often approaching the foot of the bed and being seen quite plainly or making its presence otherwise felt; or as a "presence" which is often or always somewhere near both by day and by night, in which case questions and sometimes prayers can be directed to it and a response may be telepathically received or a voice heard. The first sort of experience is an occasional one, it occurs only a few times in the narrator's life; the second sort of experience is commonplace. Both occur principally at times of crisis, particularly sickness or distress. Parents are the most common visitants, especially mothers; husbands are the next most frequent. Other relatives—children, aunts, brothers and sisters, and grandparents—are also quite common. Less material manifestations do occur (smoke, the smell of flowers, voices, disembodied faces), but these are not frequent. The dead are thought to have quite substantial powers of communication and to exist alongside the living rather than to return from a separate place.

A brief folklore history of "witnesses" will be attempted in chapter 5. Meanwhile, this one will conclude with a discussion of forbidden experiences and taboo beliefs.

DELVING

As we have seen, many of the Manchester women believed themselves to be "a little bit psychic." In general, psychic powers were approved of because they fitted into an ethic based on religious and social traditions, in particular on a concept of the "proper" role of women. Of all their values, intuition, other-person-centeredness, and order were very highly esteemed. These values were echoed, too, in their taxonomy of supernatural encounters. "Ghosts" and "hauntings" were feared because they were malevolent, purposeless, intrusive, and dangerous, and the women tried to disbelieve them if they could. Visitations from the family dead, however, being benevolent, purposeful, orderly, and intuitive experiences, were a solid part of their belief system. It is not surprising, therefore, to find that the women were very much opposed to two "psychic" practices which one would otherwise have thought to be harmless enough—reading fortunes for friends and going to seances.

Deliberate prying into the future is taken very seriously because it involves exploiting God-given powers for trivial or selfish ends. Psychic powers are regarded as a "gift" in both senses of the word—they are both a talent and an unsolicited handout (see Bennett 1995). I collected very few stories in which women make physical preparations in response to a warning or omen—a woman who has a premonition that visitors will call bakes some extra cakes, two women agree not to talk to each other because the psychic one has dreamt that they have had a quarrel, a mother waits at home because she is confident that she will hear that her daughter has been involved in an accident—that's all. Most often, it is merely psychological preparation that the foreknowledge provides: before he steps on a mine a sister "sees" her brother with "his leg all shrivelled up"; a wife "sees" the accident her husband has been involved in; an aunt has a dream that her nephew has been blinded in the war, and so on.

Psychic powers are specially tailored to the traditional female role, because they do not demand action but patience, watchfulness, and knowing compliance. Properly used, these abilities convey the power to deal with major life events on the terms that are most approved of by their peers. However, to use the gift for gain, or to "delve" into the supernatural, corrupts the gift. Five stories told about amateur fortune-telling sessions form a coherent and convincing pattern. They feature women who are, as they say, "a little bit psychic," telling fortunes for their family or friends. In

every case the result is dreadful. Rose, a married woman in her sixties, plays with a ouija board and has to undergo surgery. Clara, a
single woman in her sixties, has her hand read by a friend and
within a year her favorite nephew dies a painful death. Geraldine,
also single and in her sixties, suffers a distressing domestic
upheaval.

In the stories below, Alma reads the cups for her mother's
friend and sees there is "no future" for her; and Rose sees consider-
ably more than she bargained for. Rose and Alma both tell a good
story and so are always worth listening to, but in addition both
firmly believe they do have special powers which can indeed be har-
nessed for either good or ill. Their personal experiences therefore
deserve serious attention. The cautionary tales they have to tell can
teach the hearer a good deal about the use and abuse of gifts:

- Now, I'll tell you one thing! When I was younger I
  used to look into teacups.

  Now, mother had a friend who was terribly superstitious, and whatever I said, she took for gospel. Things
  did happen that way, but a lot of it didn't. But I know,
  the last time she asked me, she said, "Oh, you must read
  my cup!" and I looked at it and I said, "Oh!" I said.
  "There's nothing there!"

  "Oh!" she said. "There must be!"

  I said, "No, there ISN'T!" I said. "Honestly," I said,
  "there's nothing there AT ALL!" and I couldn't see a—

  Well, she was very, very offended about this, and I
  said, "No, there isn't," and when I came home, Mother
  "Oh!" she said. "Why didn't you tell her something?"

  I said, "Look, Mother! There was no future for her.
  None at ALL!"

  She said, "There must have been!"

  I said, "There WASN'T."

  I said, "I couldn't see a THING in that cup," I said,
  "and I got a queer feeling when I picked it up," I said.
  "There WASN'T ANYTHING THERE!"

  Do YOU KNOW! That next week, we were out, and we
  met a friend, and she said, "Oooh! Did you know about

so-and-so?" She'd been taken ill. She'd had a stroke, and she only lasted three days. The next thing we knew, my mother was going to her funeral. WELL NOW, that was the last time that EVER— (Alma)

• What do you want me to tell you?
[G. B.: Tell me how you think you're psychic.]
Because I know what's going to happen. I've got a pretty good idea, yeah. How do I know? Inside there [touches her head], and the fact also I've been able to tell fortunes by cards, and I was able to read cups, reading tea-leaves, and this was oh, forty, fifty years ago. I was young. I was in my teens then, you see, and I frightened myself to death. So I said, "NO WAY!" So I left the tea-leaf business alone.

When I was married, and we'd been married Lord knows how long. The war interrupted, so of course we never had any children till 1947. Now, in that summer of '47, I used to tell all fortunes by cards.
[G. B.: What's this? Tarot cards?]
No, no. PLAYING cards. Each card has a meaning and all the cards together spell out a message.

ANYWAY! I was about six or seven months pregnant and we go down to see my husband's aunt, and she was a great believer in the cards, and they have one son. Now, he was in a very good way of business. He was quite a top notch in Rolls-Royce.

Anyway! We got down there on the Saturday afternoon and there was Auntie Edie, Uncle Bernard, who are my husband's aunt and uncle, myself (complete with lump, of course!), and my husband, and Cousin Charlie met us at Chesney station, with Rolls-Royce, of course, naturally, and took us to his house.

So, we had a terrific thunderstorm in the afternoon, so, to pass the time away, Charlie and his wife said, "Let's tell our fortunes, Rose!" So I said, "Oh, OK, then," never thinking anything about it, and they got the cards out and we started, you know, and ALL I could tell her was that ALL I could see and all I could smell ALL I COULD SMELL . . . was FLOWERS and all I could see was a coffin SITTING there in the HALL on a BIER.

Now, it was a beautiful house, with a great big square hall, you see. There's a lounge at the front, and there's a dining room and there's a morning room, and there's this, that, and the other, you see.

Went to bed at night. Everybody laughed! They thought, "Oh, she's pregnant," you see. So we went to bed at night, like, and I kept crying and my husband said to me, "What the hell's the matter with you?" He says, "I can't understand you!" I said, "I want to go home! All I can see— I can ALL smell flowers and all I can see is a coffin and it's on a bier in that hall." He said, "Oh, don't be silly, Rose! You'll be all right. Get off to sleep."

NO SLEEP FOR ME!

We went home on the Sunday and Auntie Edie said to me going home on the train, "What was the matter with you yesterday, Rose?" So I told her, so I said, "There's a COFFIN. There's a FUNERAL in that house, you know." She says, "Is there?" I says, "Yes." I says, "I don't know who it is, but it's definitely in that house!"

So anyway, I think it would be July 19.

Now, in the August of '47, the great-nephew, he was fourteen years old, their only son. Their only child, everything planned and a brilliant scholar. He came over to see his Auntie Edie and contracted polio, and in three weeks he was dead, yes, AND HIS COFFIN STOOD ON A BIER IN THE HALL.

It so affected me, I said, "Never again will I tell a fortune!" FRIGHTENED me to DEATH! I said, "No!" (Rose)

To seek knowledge of unknown, and perhaps forbidden, things is suspect enough. You will see more than you bargained for and retribution will surely follow. To seek such knowledge through the agency of others—especially a professional agency—is really dangerous. It is not surprising therefore that the Manchester

"Alas, Poor Ghost!"

women have an almost universal apprehension about anything that smacks of spiritualism. Even praying to the dead and invoking their help may be wrong, as a story told by Winifred, a widow in her sixties, shows. In desperation, she prays to her dead father to help her husband. The father appears to her and the cause of the husband's illness is diagnosed and he is cured. But, despite the outcome, Winifred would "never do it again." Her father "looked weird" and seemed angry with her for bringing him back:

- [G. B.: Do you believe it's possible for the dead to come back at all?]
  I do. I believe it. My family don't, but I do, yeah.
  But I'll give you an idea.
  Once we were in Spain on holiday to a camp for five weeks and Bill started, my husband started getting terrible headaches, and we were all swimming, and he got friendly with some Scottish people and we all went swimming and that, and Bill got one of his headaches, and he couldn't see where he was going so they helped him in, and that night I was so shocked, instead of asking God to help, which he does do, I asked my dad, and as I say [I was] very close to my dad, and in my dream, maybe I was dreaming, he came back but he didn't want to come back. He really looked weird, you know, he was— He didn't say anything, but he was a bit cross with me, as I thought, for bringing him back, if you know what I mean.
  [G. B.: And you did actually see him in this sort of dream?]
  I did, yes, because he looked very unhappy, and I'd never do it again. No! Because I think once you go you're rested and that, and I think in one way you're so happy you don't want to come back. This is what I think.
  So, that's the only experience I've had.
  Anyway, he had to have an operation on his head, and he was OK afterwards, and he was in neurosurgery for two months. He had hit the side of his head with a box and he didn't remember doing it, being greengrocers. It was inside and it bled. (Winifred)

If even praying is suspect, spiritualism must be really threatening. It is delving in its most blatant form, and it also challenges the women's firmest beliefs about contact with the dead. If the dead can be summoned at will by strangers and have no purpose for their appearance but to answer foolish questions at the whim of a medium, then they cannot be the sort of intuitively apprehended community of carers that the Manchester women envisage. Indeed, they must begin to take on some of the qualities of the feared "ghosts." As Jane says in the story below, "It is the work of the devil."

- When I was in business, I used to do that [read the cups], and I had a funny experience.

    I was reading the cup and I said to one girl, "Ooh!" I said. "There's a little black girl in here!" and both the other girls said, there were about five of us, friends together in the old days, and she said, "What about going to the spiritualist's tonight?" So we said, "Oh, yes" and we went, but we didn't know what we were going in for! It was a developing circle for mediums, and however—

    "Ooh!" they said. "All take hands, friends." They turned off the lights and I got the giggles and I couldn't stop laughing.

    The lady on the door, the medium on the— "Keep on laughing, friend. You've brought that little black girl with you," and I giggled all the while. I couldn't stop, and she described my grandfather to me. He was a marvellous musician, played every instrument, and my friends said, "Oh, let's go home! Oooh, come on, let's go!" and they had one of these dark stoves, black stove with a pipe sticking up, and in a little while a woman jumped up and banged her head on this thing, and they had to bring some man in from outside, I don't know who he was, to massage her for about half an hour before she came to.

    It frightened me to death, and I thought, "Oh, it's just as the Bible says, possessed with devils!" and I went to see my grandma just after that and I told her, you know, that this lady said that this gentleman who was so musical would be— there was an old lady and he would be waiting for her and would guide her when she came to pass away. I told my grandma this.

Well, she jumped on me. She said, "I've never heard such rubbish!" she said. "I can get there myself! I can get there myself, I don't want any other help! Don't go to that place any more. It's the work of the devil." (Jane)

It is for reasons like this the Manchester women engage in contorted logic to differentiate their private beliefs about contact with the dead from this public, but antipathetic, system.

- I'm R.C., you see, and we believe that, yes, spirits do come back but not in the way spiritualists think. It's not spirits, but souls— (Norah)

- I don't know whether one can go deeper into it, I think one may get bogged down in spiritualism and that kind of thing, which I do not believe in. I don't think one should try to recall dead people. (Bessie)

However, in spite of the anxiety and taboos, a number did admit that they had visited a medium at least once in their lives.

There are fourteen accounts of such visits in all and, judging by these, the activity seems harmless enough. According to these stories, the medium merely discusses the relationship between the sitter and the one she wishes to contact, makes prosaic predictions about future events or pronouncements about the sitter or the dead relative, diagnoses disease, or says that a dead relative has a (usually trivial) message for the sitter. Nevertheless, the accounts are very defensive ones. Half of them begin with explanations or disclaimers such as:

- Well, talking about the one and only seance I was ever persuaded to go to— It was just after my mother died. I absolutely adored my mother and I was just in the mood to make any sort of contact. (Elisabeth)

- When I lost Miriam I went, as we all do, well, like some of us do, to see a spiritualist. (Audrey)

- I lost a brother in the war and I went to— Gosh! I've forgotten what you call them now— a seance. It was fashionable, I think, after the war, you know. (Doreen)

Visits to mediums are excused as being a youthful group activity, or an experiment contemplated because of family beliefs or connections, or because seances were a fashion. Speakers stress that they have been only once, or were persuaded to go, or went to please their daughters or aunts. No one confesses to going because she believes in spiritualist doctrine or ceremony.

The stories themselves are often humorous or cautionary:

- This is about my aunt, my mother's sister. She went into everything very fully, not cautious and level-headed like my mother. She went and had her spirit guides drawn for her by an artist, a medium, and one of them was a sadistic-looking nun and one was a red Indian, and she had one of these portraits in each of her bedrooms, and the one in my bedroom was the sadistic-looking nun, and I said, "You can take that down, before I'll sleep in there!" (Hilda)

Alternatively, and more interestingly, they may be made into evaluative life reviews, so that the focus of the account is turned away from the seance and on to the psychology of the sitter. A story told by Margot, a single woman over sixty, is a fine example of this type of transmutation. She focuses first on her subjective response to the experience and then uses it to explore the relationship between an invalid mother and the unmarried daughter who cares for her. She begins with a lengthy dissociative introduction:

- I once had a most remarkable experience. I went with a gang of girls I worked with in the office at the time to a spiritualist's meeting, which I don't go in for at all, because I firmly believe that if there are any spirits around, they should be left in peace. I don't want any-body whom I knew or loved sort of dragged back to—

Margot then goes on to give a brief account of the seance, again stressing aspects of her attitude that separate her from "spiritu-alists." She says, for example, that, though she did not go intending to "scoff" at the proceedings, she was in a mood to take precautions against being cheated (such as sitting apart from the friends she had gone with). Thus she establishes her credentials as a "scientific" observer rather than an involved participant. Next, she stresses aspects of the seance that were unexpected—the "spiritualist lady" came in "very bright and cheerful, not a bit glum or anything."

These contrasts are the frame for an experience which "shook me to my foundations first go off." The medium detects the related-ness of Margot and her friends immediately and announces that there is no way she can reach such unbelievers. However, she tells Margot that she is wholly dominated by her mother and memories of her mother. This account constitutes the first half of her story. The second half then goes into a discussion of her relationship with her mother, and the focus is turned away from the seance experience and on to interpersonal relationships and the ties of love and duty. Thus the nature of both the experience and the story have been changed. The taboo has been removed by the application of proper morality: like accounts of visitations, this narrative becomes a story about relationships, love, and caring.

SUMMARY

One of the particular interests of the Manchester study was being able to establish that, in a typical community in Britain today, the experience of seeing a ghost (or at least the phrase "seeing a ghost") is restricted to malevolent and purposeless manifestations. Trying deliberately to contact the dead or recall them to this world is taboo, yet at the other end of the spectrum from "ghosts" the women have an informal belief in a variety of friendly and pur-poseful visitations from dead members of the family.

In the next chapter we will look at the experience of bereave-ment and the phenomenon of "sensing the presence" of the dead to see what connections there may be with witness traditions.

Chapter 3

Witnesses, Bereavement, and the Sense of Presence

(with Kate Bennett)

WITNESSES

In the previous chapter we saw that the Manchester women believed dead family members might witness their distress and come to their rescue in times of crisis. Occasionally the witness would approach the foot of the bed at night; more often they were experienced as being "with" them or "beside" them in their daily life. Problems and prayers could be directed to them. They might be "sensed," heard, smelt, seen; very occasionally they might even touch or be touched by the percipient (see appendix 5).

There were eight stories, however, which have not been discussed so far, in which the speaker did not interpret her experience in terms of "witnesses," though they were offered as proof of the soul's survival after death. Together as a group, these eight stories show the dead in rather an idiosyncratic light: they smoke, for example, or tuck people up in bed, cough, study the sleeper, or simply walk round a door. However, they are the most poignant of all. The two below are typical:

- My little boy was drowned in the brook, did you not know? Well, I can tell you about that. I can tell you about what happened after with that. I prayed— I had— I was very, very ill, and I lay in bed one night and I said, "Please, God, just let me see him!" and he walked round the door, and I was fully awake. This is perfectly true. I was fully awake, and he came round the door, and he smiled at me, and I said, "Were you pushed, Bob, or were you— did you fall in?" and he didn't say a word, and then

I wasn't satisfied with that. I said, "Please, God," praying to God, "please let me touch him!" and I'd friends in the village, the butcher's shop opposite the cinema, and I was in bed again and he came. I said, "Please let me touch him!" and I don't know whether I was dreaming or not, but he came in front of me at their house above the butcher's shop, and he stood in front of me as he often did, and I used to stroke him under the chin. He was a gorgeous-looking little boy. He'd blond curls.

[G. B.: How old was he?]

Eight and a half, and I just touched his cheeks. Like I always did, put my hand under his cheeks, you know, and held him close to me and he was there and I did it, and I said too—What else did I ask for? My wishes were granted. It was three wishes, and I can't think what the other one was, can't think what the other— But it— I thought it was absolutely wonderful.

[G. B.: Sort of like a miracle.]

It WAS a miracle. It was a miracle TO ME. IT WAS A REAL MIRACLE, because it helped a lot to me to have my wishes granted. (Laura)

• Again, I've proof of that. My grandmother who I said I lived with as a child— I always had the habit, ALWAYS, that I had a bedroom when I was at my grandfather's house and from time to time I would remove and go and live back with my grandfather because he liked me to do that, you see, and I always slept in the bedroom I had as a child, and my grandmother always, ALWAYS, when I was in bed the last thing she did was always to come into the bedroom and sort of tuck me up in bed when I was lying there, and I FELT this whenever I went back to that house. I always felt that someone came into the bedroom when I was in bed. Not a frightening thing, a good thing, a comforting sort of thing.

[G. B.: Yes, very nice, very nice.]

Oh, yes, it was. It was! There's nothing frightening about anything like that, I don't think. I sort of had the

sensation of the door opening, because she always liked
the bedroom doors closed, you see, and I always had the
feeling that the bedroom door was being opened and
closed, and— Nothing frightening about her. (Clara)

In *Traditions of Belief* the key to such experiences was sought
in the psychology of grief and mourning, and some of the relevant
literature was briefly explored (Bennett 1987, 85–88). Since then,
interest in death-related studies, medical aspects of grief, and
bereavement counselling have all burgeoned and there is now a
wealth of research to discuss (see Averill and Nunley 1993, 77).
Since then, too, my daughter has focused her research into life-
styles of older people on the experiences of widows, and she has
embarked on a major study in the Leicester[1] area of the English
East Midlands. The majority of the narratives used to illustrate the
discussions in this chapter are taken from the first stage of this
research, which was designed as a holistic, qualitative study of the
experience and effects of bereavement on older women's lives.
This chapter is therefore a joint presentation. The methodology is
discussed in appendix 1.

We begin by discussing in a general way some recent literature about bereavement, and presenting the personal experience
of the Leicester widows. We have chosen to do this at some length
because bereavement is obviously a necessary context for any discussion of traditions about visitations from the dead. The more
one can appreciate what it is like to be bereaved, the better one
can understand (though not, we would stress, "explain" in any
mechanistic way) the sorts of experience discussed in this book.

Later, we go on to talk more specifically about what is usually
referred to in the literature as the "sense of presence": that is, the
feeling that the dead person is still with one in some sort of way.
The two narratives with which we began could be interpreted as
examples of this phenomenon. The one which follows (taken from
the Manchester research) is more clearly so:

- I don't know whether you would call it a superstition
  or— but I do believe it's very close to you at times of
  trouble or anything.

[G. B.: Some people say that their mothers particularly—]

Particularly my mother. I feel her presence, and I will say this: after she died, it was quite twelve months before I felt that her presence was no longer in the house. I felt she was there in some form or other and her bedroom seemed to be full of her for quite a long time, nearly twelve months afterwards, and then all of a sudden— We went away for the— well, the second holiday afterwards, and I came back, and the room was empty, and now, I've never told anyone else before. But it was very strong. But she was with me all that long time and then she was gone. She was gone. (May)

In order to follow up the discussion about the "sense of presence" in *Traditions of Belief*, a question was inserted at my request into the Leicester questionnaire at the planning stage.

Thirteen (possibly fourteen; see Mrs. T's[2] answer below) of the seventeen Leicester women who were asked the "presence" question[3] had had the experience or still had it. Only three had never had it or said they could not remember ever having had it. All knew exactly what was meant by the phrase, and it seems that the feeling might persist for many years. The three negative answers came from the two women who had been widowed longest (twenty-five and twenty-six years) and one of the three women who had been widowed twenty years. Though the literature suggests that it is common for the feeling to persist for a long time, up to ten years has previously been the longest time suggested as far as we are aware (see Rees 1971). Clearly this is an underestimate. Perhaps the cutoff point should be more realistically put at fifteen to twenty years. Our discussion will first present the phenomenon as described in the psychological and sociological literature, then show how the Leicester widows responded when asked whether they had ever sensed their dead husband's presence.

But first we need to discuss the experience of bereavement itself.

"Alas, Poor Ghost!"

In an essay of 1917, "Mourning and Melancholia," Sigmund Freud noted the similarities between the "normal" grief of mourning and the "pathological" grief of depression, or as he termed it "melancholia." Though the essay was primarily concerned with depression and not with bereavement, it is nowadays valued for its identification of four features of normal grief. These are profoundly painful dejection, inability to adopt new love objects, listlessness and turning away from activities not associated with the deceased, and loss of interest in the outside world. Freud saw mourning as the process whereby survivors overcame their grief by withdrawing from the deceased emotionally and learning to redirect their affection elsewhere: "The testing of reality, having shown that the loved object no longer exists, requires that all libido [ie. affection] shall be withdrawn from . . . this object. . . . [W]hen the work of mourning is completed the ego becomes free and uninhibited again" (quoted in Sanders 1989, 26).

The outlines of a similar model may be seen in the work of the "father" of bereavement research, psychologist Erich Lindemann. His 1944 study, "The Symptomatology and Management of Acute Grief"—still cited as "one of the best accounts of the syndrome of grief" (Sanders 1989, 12)—was based on the personal accounts of 101 people who had recently lost a close relative, some of them in a horrendous fire at the Cocoanut Grove nightclub in Boston, Massachusetts. He treated grief as a psycho-medical condition the symptoms of which needed to be "managed." Broadly speaking, Lindemann's approach, and particularly his phrase "grief work," are both still influential, especially amongst bereavement counsellors. According to Lindemann, those who have suffered a personal loss must learn to untie the bonds of love, to readjust to an environment in which the dead person is missing, and to form new relationships (Lindemann 1944, 143). The sign of a "pathological" grief reaction is that the mourner gets stuck in one of the early destructive phases and fails to move on at the appropriate time to the later reconstructive phases. After eight to ten sessions with a psychiatrist over a period of four to six weeks, however,

Lindemann thought "it was ordinarily possible to settle an uncomplicated and undistorted grief reaction" (ibid., 144).

The assumption in this work is that grief has recognizable emotional, behavioral, and psychological characteristics, and that grieving people will "recover" from it in due course by passing through a number of observable stages. Both Freud and Lindemann saw mourners as moving from a period of desolation and chaos through withdrawal from the lost loved one to the ability to make new ties. In the same tradition, early researchers such as Otto Fenichel saw bereavement as consisting of two stages: first a process whereby the bereaved person takes the deceased into him/herself, and secondly a stage in which they let them go; George Pollock saw the process of mourning as a movement from initial disequilibrium to the reestablishment of equilibrium; and George Engel posited six stages: shock and disbelief, developing awareness, restitution, resolving the loss, idealization, and outcome (for a discussion, see Sanders 1989, 27–35).

This sort of approach has been commonplace in bereavement studies until very recently. It underlies not only the work of psychoanalysts, but also those who use other mainstream approaches such as attachment theory or medical and social transition models (see, for example, Bowlby 1961; Hoyt 1980–81; Parkes 1986; Weiss 1982). As a recent writer puts it: "Phases of grieving have been reported to occur with some reliability in all grieving that eventually moves to recovery" (Weiss 1993, 279). However, it received particular impetus from the publication of Elisabeth Kübler-Ross's very influential book *On Death and Dying* (1970) which presents a five-stage model of the grief of dying patients.

A typical modern stage model of the grieving process can be found in Catherine Sanders's handbook, *Grief: The Mourning After: Dealing with Adult Bereavement* (1989). The whole of part 2 is given to "The Phases of Bereavement." It not only draws on her own research, but it synthesizes the work of a great many scholars in the field; its comprehensiveness means that it can be taken as representative of the effects noted by a wide variety of researchers who adopt stage theories of bereavement. Briefly, phase 1 is "shock" (marked by disbelief, confusion, restlessness, feelings of

"Alas, Poor Ghost!"

unreality, preoccupation with thoughts of the deceased). Phase 2 is "awareness of loss" (separation anxiety, conflicts, yearning, anger, guilt, sleep disturbances, sensing the presence, dreaming). Phase 3 is "conservation and withdrawal" (despair, fatigue, a weakened immune system, obsessional review). The fourth stage is "healing" (the bereaved person assumes control, restructures his or her identity, relinquishes previous roles, and begins to sleep better and to be more resistant to physical illness). The fifth and final phase is "renewal," in which the bereaved person may expect to find a new self-awareness, accept responsibility, and learn to live without the one they have lost. The time the complete process lasts varies from individual to individual. Some may accomplish the whole cycle in just a month, others may require years (Sanders 1989, 45–108).

The Leicester study was not designed to test stage theories of grief but it does provide snapshots of three periods in the course of a bereavement. After initial orienting questions about how long they had been married and what a typical day in their married life had been like, the interviewer encouraged the widows to talk, first about the time immediately following their husband's death, then what it was like a year on, and finally what it is like now. The technique was to invite narratives rather than to ask very specific questions and expect snappy replies, so it is sometimes difficult to tell how long after the death of their husband some of the events and feelings they are describing took place.[4] Nevertheless, it is interesting to note that, though there is not much evidence of a steady progression from shock through denial to withdrawal as the models predict, the Leicester widows give a very vivid picture of what it feels like to be bereaved in the early weeks or months corresponding to Sanders's phases 1 to 3. Likewise, "stages 4 and 5" are observable in the narratives, at least in the very broad sense that there comes a time when the widow is able and ready to start to rebuild her life (though again it is not easy to distinguish between the two stages, and the model predicts that the process is both more complete and more complex than the Leicester accounts indicate).

Among the effects the Leicester widows report in the early days, those attributed to shock are very common. They say they felt "dazed," "in a complete dream," "in a complete fog," "numb," "shattered," "lost," "on automatic pilot," "like a zombie." Many report that they cannot remember the early days at all. Some say, "I didn't know where I was really," or "I don't think I knew what I was doing." Some cannot believe, or will not accept, the death. Some say they were indifferent to life, they did not eat, they "gave up," lost interest in everything, could not concentrate. One said she felt betrayed and "let down" by her husband; another was angry because her husband "didn't deserve" to die. Among emotions often reported in the first weeks and months were anxiety and nervousness, guilt, loneliness, confusion, emptiness, tearfulness. They also felt "ragged and drained," exhausted, withdrawn, mutilated ("like half a person"), and resentful ("why me?"). Some brooded over the death; some were afraid to go to bed at night, while others lost all sense of fear (one lady reports taking cycle rides through the city at 3 A.M., another says she "did a lot of mad things"); three became very dependent on their children; one became "hard and bitter"; two were physically ill; one had panic attacks; and one could not cope at all. Three could not bear to be in the house and literally wandered the streets; two sold their houses straight away; four immediately went on holiday with family or friends or fled to a relative's house; eight displayed the classic "flight into activity" pattern of bereavement literature, filling the day with hasty and ill-considered activity, decorating the house, changing the furniture, digging the garden, anything to take their mind off their sorrow.[5] Many withdrew from social contact:

- I didn't want to talk to anybody, and, I mean, you've probably gathered, I'm a fairly outgoing person, but I wanted to shut myself away. On the bus, I used to take a book, and if I saw anybody I'd say, "I hope you don't mind, I'm going to have a cigarette upstairs and I'm reading something important." I couldn't bear to talk about the weather and casual things. It was too trivial, after what had happened. (Mrs. P, transcript, 7)

Initially most of the Leicester widows seem to have had high levels of support from family and friends, but that soon dropped off, leaving many socially isolated. Old acquaintances were embarrassed by their own inability to find anything appropriate to say and hurried by them in the street; married women friends began to avoid them, or so they thought. Being with couples was difficult, seeing people in pairs in the street was overwhelmingly painful. One lady said:

- I can always remember in the early days I used to say, "Even the birds are in twos!" I can always remember saying to myself, "Oh, the birds are flying about in twos," and I used to really sort of resent being on my own to begin with. (Mrs. F, transcript, 23)

Everything upset them—photographs, memories, the behavior of others—and life was extremely difficult.

Among the twenty interviews there is one particularly graphic account of this painful state and the subsequent gradual rebuilding of a shattered life:

- The awful thing about bereavement is, other things are repairable . . . you can build. . . . You can do it with just about everything else, but death is so final, and there isn't anybody in the world, not even [laughs] God himself, can do anything to bring it back, you know, to change it. Nobody can change it. So, it's— it's handling that. That's the difficult bit. Knowing it's so permanent, so definite. . . . And every time the phone rings it's going to be him, every time somebody comes to the door— 'cause then you had then a lot of visitors which is good for you— and this all happens for a fortnight and then, they stop. Nothing happens then. People stop ringing, people stop calling and then you're suddenly, completely, just you. . . . You're completely drained of everything. Your emotions are so badly damaged, you know, so hurt. . . .

  But one feeling that I definitely remember . . . I felt like . . . I was going down this road, going down this road. This is Forever Road, and you know— and it just goes on forever with the sun at the other end, and it's forever, and it's just as I want it, and we're going to do so many lovely things because Stan is going to retire, and I was retiring at the same time as him—. You know, this lovely road that you're going to go down is there, and then suddenly it's just like a great prison door. There's a great, thick, big, black door there in front of you, and it's just like somebody's standing there and said, "You can go down THAT road, you can go down THAT road. But you're never going to go down THIS road ever again." You stand there, you stand there, and that's where you seem to stand for a long, long time . . .

So, you know, you're in this complete turmoil and then you suddenly— I can't tell you how long it is, how long it is before you decide,— but suddenly you decide, "Well, I know I've got to go down one of those roads!" and you start to sort of feel yourself, and you start to go out a little bit and go somewhere. You know, go and do something different— and the one thing you do find is you have to find yourself, because you've been two people. . . .

[*Interviewer:* So it's something about learning to be single?]

Having to be single. Learning to be just you, yes, and to be a single person. All the time you're doing this, your partner's still coming back. It's only temporary. He's gone, unfortunately he's had to go away for a long time but, you know, one day it's all going to come back to normal. . . .

I didn't paint for six months after Stan died [Mrs. A is an accomplished amateur artist]. I just couldn't, I just couldn't bring myself, and then one day . . . one morning I woke up and I said, "Do you know, Stan would want this. He'd want you to paint, Stan would— he knew you were painting. He gave you a lot of encouragement." And I picked up a brush again and I was away. . . .

"Alas, Poor Ghost!"

You must do an awful lot of thinking and— the mind develops itself, you know, in a different way. It must do because, as I say, you keep waking up, say in the morning, and you suddenly decide it's time you did so and so and it's time you did this and it's time you did that. So, it doesn't JUST happen, it GRADUALLY happens. You think about all these different things, and . . . I found that I've got to sort of fill my life. You've got to fill it. It's got to be full. Suddenly, you know, a bit of this cloud has lifted. You've come out of the fog. You've actually come out of the fog. This big door has gone away and you realize now there's those two roads. . . . The choice is yours and you know that's it, so you take these— you go down any of these— you know, it's almost like blood veins. You've lost all that feeling that, you know, that you want to die because that's just a short a short-lived— If I put, say three months on that, now don't say "Why I'm putting that [time limit] on?" because I haven't a clue! That just came, but for that it could be six months, a year. But that seems to dwindle, you seem to find that you could— cope with being alive.
[*Interviewer*: Right. But it's coping as opposed to enjoying?]
Oh yes, yes, yes, yes, yes.
[*Interviewer*: Surviving rather than—]
It's a battle to survive, yeah. A battle to survive, and like this I was telling you, there's always this great hole inside that hurts, and I felt, you know, it didn't matter what you did, it's there, it was there. So I felt all these things I was doing, as if I was building a pattern, a life round it. I couldn't— you can't ever— fill it, but you build a life round, and that gives a little bit of security. You're starting to feel a bit more secure and you're doing things on your own. . . .

I feel, considering the situation I'm in, I'm coping with it. Yes, I feel I'm coping with it well. Whether I am or not—. But everybody else thinks I am, and I think everybody— well, I've had it said to me. Now this might sound like I'm bragging but I'm not. People have said to me, "I wish I could handle it like you" and I think, "Well, I don't know [laughs], I don't know that I'm handling it that well. They don't know how I feel inside." But I do, I do tend to put up a very good— and I don't do it deliberately. I think there is a lot of me out there. A lot of me out there. It's not— I'm not hiding anything. It is mostly me. Yes, I am me now. I have found me, though I'm no different to the other me, though I'm my own me— own me. Does that make any sense to you? . . . I can't tell you how long ago that was, but I suddenly remember that— feeling, when I was single, "This is me. Nobody else is doing this." (Mrs. A [widowed nine years], transcript, 7–34)

Mrs. A has plainly made what stage models of bereavement would call a successful recovery, rebuilding her life as an independent person after the destructive desolation of loss. Similar processes can be found in many other accounts. Just over half of the Leicester widows speak of new confidence and independence, new friends and hobbies and skills, an active social life, and holidays abroad. They claim they have a good quality of life and sometimes speak of the pleasures of what they call "selfishness" (in other words, pleasing themselves). Though it is difficult to detect an ordered progression through several distinct phases in their stories, one can usually see a movement from numbness and disorder, through a purposeful reconstruction or rediscovery of self, to functional competence. Nevertheless, we think the Leicester narratives show that stage theories have weaknesses which are currently often overlooked.

The first, and perhaps most obvious, is that they assume a uniformity of experience—that everyone is the same and feels the same. A moment's reflection shows this cannot be the case. The psychiatrist Colin Murray Parkes, one of the foremost British grief researchers, while himself using stage theories in his early work, has cogently observed that:

"Alas, Poor Ghost!"

Grief is an emotion that draws us toward something or someone that is missing. It arises from awareness of a discrepancy between the world that is and the world that "should be." This raises a problem for researchers because, though it is not difficult to discover the world that is, the world that should be is an internal construct; hence each person's grief is individual and unique. Two women who have lost husbands are not the same. One may miss her husband greatly, while the other's grief may arise less from her wish to have her husband back (for she never did like him as a person) than from the loss of the status and power that she achieved in marrying an important man. Clearly grief is not a unitary phenomenon. (1993, 242)

The Leicester accounts show this very clearly. The women's responses to bereavement run the whole gamut from breakdown to gladness. At one extreme, some pine for their lost mates for very many years; at the other extreme, one widow who was asked what was the first thing she did after her husband died said she took a bath. "When he did die," she said, "I'd shed all my tears in those two years I'd been taking care of him, and it was a relief to me, because life was so hard."

Another problem is that stage models measure "recovery" by the degree of independence and reintegration into the community,[6] though social engagement is actually a poor measure of quality of life. The Nottingham Longitudinal Study of Activity and Ageing (NLSAA) found that, whilst levels of social participation remained stable following a bereavement, depression increased and morale decreased for up to eight years (K. M. Bennett 1996; Bennett and Morgan 1992). Other researchers have noted that "it must not be assumed that the development of new relationships is always necessary or beneficial for widows. Social interaction is not synonymous with social support" (Prosterman 1996, 195). Indeed, it can often create more problems than it solves (Rook 1984; see also Rook 1989).

The biggest problem, however, may be the concept of "recovery" itself, which is built in by nature of the analogy to physical trauma:

On the whole [wrote Parkes in an early work which exemplified the medical model of grief], grief resembles a physical injury more closely than any other type of illness. The loss may be spoken of as a "blow." As in the case of physical injury, the "wound" gradually heals; at least, it usually does. But occasionally complications set in, healing is delayed, or a further injury reopens a healing wound. . . . (1986, 25)

Parkes himself is not judgmental about recovery, but a tone of certainty, almost of accusation, sometimes creeps into other discussions. In particular, perhaps because they were initially designed to distinguish "normal" from "morbid" grief, stage models often pathologize a deep and lasting grief. The quotation within the quotation below is taken from Parkes's work, but the interpretation is the author's own:

Atypical or morbid grief reactions are not qualitatively different from normal grief responses; they differ only in intensity and duration. For example, statements like "I miss him every moment of the day; I want my husband every minute of the day but neither you nor anybody else can give him back to me" (Parkes 1972) would be considered normal bereavement responses if made a few weeks after the death. If they were made one-and-a-half or nine years after the death, they would be identified as morbid or abnormal grief responses. (Schulz 1978, 149)

This sort of attitude is neither helpful nor realistic. A further difficulty is that the very same women who have apparently reintegrated themselves successfully and become functioning members of society again (and whose "wound" is thus judged to have "healed" according to the usual criteria) nevertheless speak of a continuing sense of loss. The "blow" remains a blow.

This is even the case for the triumphantly well-adjusted Mrs. A:

- . . . it's just there, and it's deep and— it just never, ever goes away. But you, you, you build this around it so that— I suppose you disguise it. But you just carry on. Life's like that, you know you've got to carry on. But I suppose it's only at times like this [like talking to the interviewer] that again— You see, you've allowed those feelings to come to the top again— and I suppose you could even tend to feel that— you perhaps pretend that they're not there now, you know. But they are— and little things spark it off, you know, and you have your little moments, on your own, that spark it off but— you just wish that it had never happened, always.

The Leicester widows have been widowed at least two years; some of them for twenty years or more. According to most stage theories, they should be "over" their grief. Nevertheless, six of them still miss their husband or are lonely without him, thirteen or fourteen still sense his presence, five still talk to him as if he were alive, five still keep a few of his clothes or possessions, two attend spiritualist meetings, two still harbor destructive emotions, one is envious of the still-married, one says nothing has changed from the first days of her bereavement, and others wake up and think he's in bed with them. Some have very limited aspirations, content to be "coping," "living from day to day," refusing to plan ahead for fear of disappointment. Mrs. P, for example, who has been widowed thirteen years and has suffered several illnesses since, summed up her hopes for the future thus: ". . . so that's all I really want out of life, to feel well and to cope, and to see my family when I can. My expectations aren't very great but I'm satisfied" (transcript, 19). The overwhelming impression is that these widows have not "recovered" from their loss as if it were a bout of chicken pox, but rather have decided, in the popular phrase, that "life goes on."

Another problem arises from the medicalization of mourning. This is the assumption that if bereavement is a sickness then the grief-stricken person must be a "patient" whose condition has to be "managed" by others (see Lindemann's title [1944]). The result of this is that control is taken away from the griever and assumed by others. Everyone is an expert except the bereaved person him or herself. Catherine Sanders's discussion of the stages of grief concludes, for example, with the comment: "a phasic model of bereavement allows caregivers[7] to determine where each grieving individual is in the overall bereavement process in order to provide the appropriate intervention for each phase" (1989, 107). The effects of such assumptions have been recently highlighted in an article written by a British social work lecturer who has himself been bereaved:

> At the time, and for some years after my daughter's death, I felt alienated by "models of grief," which seemed so clear-cut and prescriptive, either in themselves, in the way they were applied, or both. There are the "stages or phases" to pass through. . . . Even time scales are indicated during which certain stages or phases had to be completed. . . . "You still sound angry" an acquaintance, a counsellor, said to me a year after Gaia's death. I was baffled by this statement, which struck me as nonsensical. . . . However, her misplaced concern raised my anxiety, because the implication was: "This is not normal . . . you should be over that feeling by now." (Footman 1998, 292)

How damaging this might become is discussed by a leading American researcher, Helena Lopata:

> Unfortunately, the stages and calendar of "normal" grieving became part of American culture. . . . What makes it problematic for the grieving person is that [American] society has very definite ideas as to normalcy and very little tolerance for behavior and emotional responses it considers inappropriate. Close associates familiar with this theory and even those in secondary relationships tend to watch for the widowed woman's "normal" movement from stage to stage, commenting to her if she is entering or exiting too early or too late for each one. This can have devastating effects, especially if she takes the progression seriously, questioning even her sanity if she is defined as off time. (1996, 102)

Echoes of this judgmental view of how long it takes to recover from bereavement can be found in the Leicester narratives too. Mrs. G, for example, reflects:

- There was too many people telling you what you should do. As I say, widows can't win. You either get people saying, if you go out, "Oh, she's getting over that quick!"— you know, the old sort of— [laughs]. "You'd have thought she'd have stayed at home a bit longer," and that sort of thing. But if you DO stay at home and be miserable and that, well they'll say, "It's time she got over that." (transcript, 15)

Such attitudes can be very hurtful, as Mrs. A recalls:

- I remember going out once and then somebody was going by, and I was really, really hurt. Because I was doing it for US. And this person turned and said, "Oh, look at you all dressed up again. Where are you gadding off to now?" And I wasn't gadding ANYWHERE, I was struggling to— I was going out because I couldn't stay IN, and I'd dressed myself up because I wanted to stay still proud, I wanted to be Mrs. A and respect myself again. Because I was always proud that he, he respected how I looked after myself, so no way was I going to let the side down. (transcript, 37)

Fortunately, recent work has begun to move away from approaches which encourage these sorts of judgmental attitudes. Leading theorists Margaret and Wolfgang Stroebe and Robert Hansson, for example, note that there have recently been "significant advances" from clinical models and that it "seems evident now that a narrow interpretation of grief as a form of mental or physical illness or debility, or as a matter of clinical concern alone . . . is no longer viable" (Stroebe, Hansson, and Stroebe 1993, 458; see also Charmaz 1980, 148–55). Stephen Shuchter and Sidney Zisook have admitted that "several features of grief, particularly those related to attachment behaviours . . . continue several years after the loss . . .

some aspects of grief work may never end for a significant proportion of otherwise normal bereaved persons" (Shuchter and Zisook 1993; for a discussion, see Lopata 1996, 101–3). Rather more liberally, Marcia Kraft Goin has argued that some people maintain a "timeless" emotional involvement with the deceased, and this is often a "healthy adaptation" to loss (Goin, Burgoyne, and Goin 1979). Nevertheless, it has to be noted that these models persist in a lot of the literature aimed at self-help or bereavement counselling (see, for example, Bowling and Cartwright 1982, 141–66; Moorey 1995, 129–47; and Sanders 1989).

Most counselling literature also fails to recognize—and this is an important omission—that some bereaved people choose to cope with their loss by dying themselves and that this is a logical way of coping with their situation. A famous epigraph by Sir Henry Wotton (1568–1639) makes this point very poignantly ("Death of Sir Albertus Moreton's Wife"):

> He first deceas'd: she for a little tri'd
> To live without him, lik'd it not, and di'd.

Men in particular often opt for this way out (see Lopata 1996, 108). One researcher notes:

> The turning point of grief is marked with a decision either to move forward— and in so doing relinquish the past as it had been lived with the deceased— or to remain in the status quo, not making changes. . . . A third choice is seldom discussed as an alternative, but is selected far more often than realized: the decision to die. Sometimes this is not a conscious decision but is more an unconscious desire, and death results from illness or accidents. (Sanders 1989, 82)

Sanders's own study in Tampa, Florida, revealed that the number of infections, diseases, and accidents was significantly higher among recently bereaved people than among the general population, and that illnesses around the anniversary of the death were common (ibid., 82–83; see also [K.M.] Bennett 1998; Parkes

"Alas, Poor Ghost!"

1964; Parkes 1986, 34–46; and Stroebe and Stroebe 1993). Nowadays, of course, grief is not recognized as a cause of death (except perhaps in fiction). But it used to be. Thus a classification of causes of death in London in 1657 lists:

Flox and Small Pox	835
Found dead in the street	9
French Pox	25
Gout	8
Griefe	10
Griping and Plague in the Guts	446
Hang'd and made away 'emselves	24

(Quoted in Parkes 1986, 34)

THE SENSE OF PRESENCE

If the bereaved person chooses to survive, they find themselves committed to what researchers Robert Hansson, Jacqueline Remondet, and Marlene Galusha call the "career of widowhood" (Hansson, Remondet, and Galusha 1993, 373–75). Helena Lopata likewise speaks of a husband's death as first moving a woman "into the temporary role of widow and then into a pervasive identity as widowed woman" (Lopata 1996, xiii). As Hansson and his colleagues note: "for many widows there is a substantial 'lifetime' still ahead" (Hansson, Remondet, and Galusha 1993, 375). Throughout this "lifetime," but especially in the first ten years, most widows find comfort in things which connect them to the dead man. The importance of possessions is emphasized again and again in the bereavement literature. A study of seventy young London widows, undertaken in 1958 by Peter Marris, for example, found that "brooding over memories, clinging to possessions" was marked in the early years (1974, 25). Shuchter and Zisook found that over 40 percent of the 350 bereaved men and women they studied in San Diego kept some of their late spouse's belongings near them for a year or more (1993, table 2.3). Parkes observed that one woman

> kept going through her husband's clothes, feeling in the pockets and gazing at them. . . . A London widow regularly wore her husband's dressing gown. . . . A thirteen

year old girl who had lost her father angered and disgusted her mother by taking his pyjama jacket to bed with her at night. Photographs, pipes, wallets, and other "close" personal possessions were often prominently displayed. . . . Favourite pieces of furniture, "his chair" for example, were objects of special reverence. (1986, 71)

Likewise, anthropologist Geoffrey Gorer noted that: "Most widows sell or give away most of their husband's possessions . . . but many keep one personal relic, his watch, his favourite blazer and the like" ([1965] 1977, 110).

The Leicester widows were no different. Over half the group produced photographs to show the interviewer, and it may be assumed that most of them had pictures of their husbands somewhere (only one says she has not "even got a picture on the wall"). Many also kept mementoes at least for a while, though there seems to come a time when a conscious decision is made to let them go:

- You have to grieve, you HAVE to grieve. I mean, my husband had traveled the world and I'd got a cabincase full of photographs. He used to take about three of everything, and I just couldn't bring it here with me [when she moved house], and I spent an entire day on the floor with this trunk which had trays which lifted out, going through photographs and tearing them up. I spent the day laughing and crying at them all. But at the end of the day I'd reduced them down to a small amount which I really wanted to keep. (Mrs. F, transcript, 10)

These mementoes are usually personal possessions of some kind, rings, watches, and service medals maybe, but most often clothes:

- He had a new anorak that he wore all the time that he was ill and it was in the hall cupboard where we keep the coats and shoes, and he'd got a silly hat, a straw hat

"Alas, Poor Ghost!"

thing that he'd bought on holiday that he used to wear when he took the dog out if it was raining, and I always used to take the mickey out of him [laughs]. It were terrible! [still laughing] Because he always kept it in this cupboard and if it were raining he always plonked it on his head and— . His coat and that hat were there and I couldn't bear to part with it because I felt as if somehow he were still around while that was there, like the old familiar things. (Mrs. D, transcript, 46–47)

One of the Leicester widows still makes regular visits to the cemetery; two visit, or have visited, mediums. Many dream of the dead man ("dreams of the past and your husband's always with you," as Mrs. I said) and most talk to him as if he were still alive. Only four of the widows said they did not recall ever having done so.

Talk is very important. As Parkes puts it, "Faced with the biggest trouble she has ever had, the widow repeatedly finds herself turning toward a person who is not there" (1993, 243). Shuchter and Zisook found that two months after the bereavement 39 percent of their respondents still talked to their dead spouse regularly. Figures declined slightly at thirteen months but still stayed above 33 percent (1993, table 2.3). Mrs. D says:

- The actual day to day knowing that somebody's there and cares about you, got a sympathetic ear if you want to talk about— you know somebody's upset you or something or you're not very well, or you know, just general affection. That's what I miss more than anything else. (Mrs. D, transcript, 27)

Photographs in particular become a focus for communication with the dead (42 percent of Shuchter and Zisook's respondents talked to their late spouse's photograph. See Shuchter and Zisook 1993, table 2.3):

- And I still talk, his photograph's behind the [?] by the way, behind the card. Yes, I still talk to him, odd times.

If things are not going right, or anything like that, and you know, specially sometimes when the garden, the things we planted— and there's very often when I am in the garden and I say to him, "You ought to be back here, you know," and, "See what's happened," [laughs] and that. I mean, I do talk to him [?]. When I go to bed, if I'm watching something on the telly I often say, "Oh, I wish you were here to watch that" [laughs], you know, and I always say goodnight to that photo when I go to bed. (Mrs. D, transcript, 42–43)

- . . . when you're in your house on your own, I'll sit and talk to him in that picture. I mean, you may think I'm daft but I do. . . . About a year or so, a year or eighteen months after, I started. You see, I didn't get that photograph until a wee while after, until my brother sent it. (Mrs. E, transcript, 11, 19)

The sense of a continued relationship is also important: "I mean sometimes I quite often say, 'Oh, I still love you,' because although he's died you don't lose feeling for the person," says Mrs. P (transcript, 24).

The post-bereavement experience that best encapsulates these themes, providing closeness, communication, and the continuation of an important relationship is what the literature calls the "illusion" or "sense" of the dead person's presence. At its weakest this is a feeling that one is somehow being watched; at its strongest it is a full-blown sensory experience. Such phenomena were alluded to in Lindemann's early study, where he attributes them to changes in the "sensorium" and cites two cases:

A patient who lost his daughter in the Cocoanut Grove disaster visualized his girl in the telephone booth calling for him and was much troubled by the loudness with which his name was called and was so preoccupied with the scene that he became oblivious of his surroundings. A young navy pilot lost a close friend; he remained a vivid part of his imagery . . . in terms of an

"Alas, Poor Ghost!"

imaginary companion. He ate with him and talked over problems with him. . . . Up to the time of the study, six months later, he denied the fact that the boy was no longer with him. (1944, 142)

Later, Marris was to find the following typical of the early stages of mourning: "inability to comprehend the loss, brooding over memories, clinging to possessions, *a feeling that the dead man is still present, expecting him home with every turn of the key in the door, and talking to him and of him as if he were still alive*" (1974, 25–26, our emphasis). Of the 72 widows Marris studied, 36 experienced a sense of the husband's presence, and 15 continued to behave as if he were still alive, a process he calls a refusal to "surrender the dead, reviving them in imagination" (ibid., 28). In the early 1970s, the *British Medical Journal* carried a survey by a Welsh family doctor which recorded an incidence of almost 50 percent post-bereavement "hallucinations" as he called them (auditory and visual) among his sample of 293 local people, and noted that he had found that they were common during the first ten years of widowhood (Rees 1971). Similarly, American researchers Richard Kalish and David Reynolds concluded that "the individual realities of a substantial proportion of residents of one urban area include interpersonal perceptions of dead persons who had returned" (1973, 220).

Since then, it has become the consensus among bereavement researchers that these sorts of experiences are commonplace.[8] In 1974, Ira O. Glick, Robert S. Weiss, and Colin Murray Parkes studied 68 widows and widowers in Boston, Massachusetts. They reported one young widow as telling her daughter, "I've always believed that Mike knows and sees everything we do, and I try to teach [my daughter] that, too, about her father. I say, 'The brightest star in heaven, that's your daddy watching you.'" Four of their respondents reported briefly seeing their husbands as if they were alive, sitting in their favorite armchair or going into another room. Many felt the presence in connection with experiences they had shared, such as getting breakfast or watching TV. The researchers concluded: "The greater part of our sample seemed to maintain some sense of their husband's presence, ranging from a vague feeling through actual hallucinatory experience, during the first two months of their bereavement" (1974, 136–37).

Psychologists have not been alone in noticing this phenomenon. British "Agony Aunt," Virginia Ironside, in her popular book *"You'll Get Over It"* quotes several accounts from literature and the media, including the personal experience of the actor George Baker:

> All my life I've felt [my father's] presence. Years after he died I was on the number 73 bus going past the Royal Albert Hall in London. In my mind my dad was sitting next to me and we were having a really good chat. Another passenger came up the stairs and I only just stopped myself remarking: "Sorry, that seat is already taken." (quoted in Ironside 1996, 155)

British anthropologist Geoffrey Gorer discovered the sense of presence when he researched his classic *Death, Grief and Mourning.* He reported that 31 of the 80 people he personally interviewed had what he called "dreams and visions" of the person they were mourning. Five of them were brave enough to challenge his interpretation and insisted they were *not* dreaming (Gorer [1965] 1977, 54). More recently, Douglas Davies's work explored the same territory. He reports that "approximately 35 per cent" of the people contacted for his 1995 survey "had gained some such sense of the presence of the dead" (1997, 154; and see Davies and Shaw 1995, table 8.13). One of the examples he gives is that of a woman whose husband had died several years previously: "[She] said that she could still feel him sometimes touch her head. She can smell his cigarettes, can feel him near and can communicate with him" (Davies 1997, 155). Davies also quotes "one of the most interesting 'literary' cases" involving the theologian J. B. Phillips and C. S. Lewis, author of the "Narnia" books:

> A few days after his death, while I was watching television [Phillips wrote], he "appeared" sitting in a chair within a few feet of me and spoke a few words . . . particularly relevant to the difficult circumstances through

which I was passing. . . . I had not been thinking of him at all. I was neither alarmed nor surprised . . . he was just here. A week later when I was in bed he appeared again . . . and repeated the same message which was very important to me at the time. . . .[9]

Davies adds, "When Phillips told these experiences to a retired bishop, the reply was, 'My dear J., this sort of thing is happening all the time'" (Davies 1997, 154).[10]

The Phillips example is one of the very few cases when someone feels the presence of someone he does not know particularly well. Davies notes that sensing the presence of a parent is the most common type of these experiences (15.4 percent); grandparents follow next (10.3 percent), then spouses (5.0 percent), siblings (2.2 percent), children (1.1 percent); and other kin (3.6 percent). One point seven percent sense the presence of friends; only 0.7 percent of his sample sense the presence of other non-kin (see Davies and Shaw 1995, table 6.14, 97).

The experience is also common among the Leicester widows, as their answers to the "presence" question show. The positive responses are printed below without comment. Readers will see that the accounts are quite varied in tone and content, but cover all the sorts of experiences thought typical. It should also be noted that these responses show that the "sense of presence" is by no means restricted to the early months of bereavement, but persists far longer than is sometimes recognized. As we noted above, the evidence from the Leicester study shows that the cutoff point may be fifteen to twenty years.

- [*Interviewer*: Can I ask you whether you felt as if he was still, you felt as if he was still around, still talking to you?]

  Still do, and I'm a very skeptical person. I'm skeptical about almost anything. But the strange thing— and he would find that probably as difficult to believe as if I said it to anybody, but yes, yes, to me he's still often around, and when I'm sometimes doing things, it's ever so strange. I'll probably decide I'm going to be— Well, it's not so much now because I know where pretty well everything is, but I know when first I started doing jobs and I was thinking, "Now how on earth— how would Stan do this?" and I'd think, "How would he tackle it?" and I'd go out to look for the whatever-it-was, and it was just as if it was almost put in my hand to do it. And you find these things extremely strange if you never believe in any of this sort of thing, but yes it did. It is, yes. (Mrs. A [widowed nine years])

- [*Interviewer:* So the year after his death, what sort of point were you at? I mean, how did you feel a year after he'd gone?]
  I still felt a bit as if it was my fault, and I still— when I used to sit and think— couldn't think where he was. I used to try and picture what he was doing and where he was. And you sit there, and then you realize, well he just can't be anywhere because he was cremated. But even now, even talking to you, I'd like to know where Bob is. But they don't exist really, do they, you see?[11]
  [*Interviewer:* Do you not feel his presence?]
  Well, I do sometimes, yes. And I sometimes like to think that he'd be pleased with how I'd coped you know, and things like that. (Mrs. B [widowed six years], transcript, 11)

- [*Interviewer:* Did you at that stage, did you still feel the presence of your husband?]
  Oh yeah.
  [*Interviewer:* Just round the house or everywhere?]
  All over.
  [*Interviewer:* Did you talk to him?]
  Yeah, yeah, and I used to say if I were looking for any-thing, "Oh, crikey! Help me!" and it's surprising, they do. You do get through it, you know, and I used to say— You'd turn round and he'd say to me, "I don't know what you're bothering to do that for! It don't need

"Alas, Poor Ghost!"

doing," and you say, "You told me it didn't need doing,"
You know, I've often felt him, often felt— his presence.
(Mrs . C [widowed five years], transcript, 14)

Mrs. C later adds, "Their spirit's still with you, in't it? It is, yeah.
Oh yeah. I don't think they ever leave you" (transcript, 18).

- [*Interviewer*: Has that been with you all the way along?
  That feeling of his presence?]
  Oh yeah, yes. I know— I mean, I can't say it's [?] definite,— but I know that he's around because, as I say,
  since I've been interested in the spiritual side, you
  know, sometimes they give you messages, and I said to
  him once— I was watching a musical show and it's
  something he would have loved, you know— and I
  said, "Oh, it's a pity you're not here to watch this," and
  I thought, "Why am I talking to him if he's not here?"
  and, anyway, I went to church [the spiritualist church]
  and this lady says, "Ooh, your husband says—" She
  says, "I've got your husband here," and she described
  him, and she says, "He says he WAS there watching the
  telly and listening to the music with you." You know,
  he must be there. He MUST be there. I mean, there's
  been one or two instances like that. At the funeral, I—
  the wreath was in the shape of a heart with roses in the
  middle, and in the card I put, "Goodnight Sweetheart,"
  you know, and this man said to me once, he said, "I've
  got this gentleman, and he says you still look back to
  the time of his passing and he doesn't want you to. He
  wants you to look forward and not grieve about what
  happened then," and he said— He talked about his
  funeral and he said, "I must've been popular. There
  were a lot there," and he says, "also he's talking about a
  heart, a heart of flowers. Did you send a wreath in the
  shape of a heart?" and I says, "Yes, I did," and he says,
  "He's saying 'Goodnight Sweetheart,'" which is what
  was on the card, you see, and he says, "And you took
  two roses, didn't you, out of that heart and you took

them home?" and I said, "Yes." I mean, I'm not trying to convert you, but I'm just telling you what happens that gives you a lift. (Mrs. D [widowed two years], transcript, 43–44)

- [*Interviewer:* Okay. Do you ever still talk to your husband or do you feel his presence around?]
  Oh yes, frequently [loud laugh]. Curse him sometimes. Erm, yes. I think— sometimes if I've done a silly thing I'll probably say something to him. Yes I do, yes. (Mrs. F [widowed twenty years], transcript, 16)

- [*Interviewer:* Have you, or do you, at any point, feel the presence of your husband? Do you ever talk to him or—?]
  Sometimes I get angry. Yes, there is that certain. It's not very often. If I go down the bottom of the garden on that seat. . . . I've looked up, and I can see my children on this patio, and I can see him on this patio, and I get very morbid . . . but yes, he does come back. I don't know what he'd think, "Good God! What have you done to the house. You've been spending all my money!" Oh yeah. (Mrs. I [widowed fifteen years], transcript, 13–14)

- [*Interviewer:* Did you still feel the presence of your husband at that stage?]
  Yes, as if he was kind of at the back of me.
  [*Interviewer:* Do you still get that?]
  Occasionally, yes I do.
  [*Interviewer:* At any specific time, or just sort of—?]
  No, any time. You couldn't say any— Probably sometimes in the garden, and he'll say, "No, you don't do it like that!" [laughs]. But apart from that, it just comes on any time, you know, and the funny thing is, my daughter's said that as well. Sometimes she can feel it. It's at the back of you or something. Just looking after us I think. (Mrs. J [widowed two years], transcript, 10–11)

- [*Interviewer:* OK. Did you continue to feel the presence of your husband once he'd gone?]
  In some things yes, but in others no. (Mrs. L [not clear how long widowed], transcript, 7)

- I mean I wake up in the night and think they're there in bed with you sometimes. It's all in the mind.
  [*Interviewer:* Do you feel the presence of your husband?]
  Occasionally, yes. (Mrs. M [widowed nine years], transcript, 18)

- [*Interviewer:* OK. Do you ever feel the presence of your husband?]
  No, I've never felt the presence. I've never seen him. . . . But I said to— when we went to the college, "I've got a feeling that we get in touch, or the presence of him is there in music." I can't explain it. He loved— Oh, he'd got such varied taste in music! And if I'm ever feeling really down, I can just put the radio on and it's— well, it's not "spooky," but I can't describe it. You can bet, two or three tunes after, there'll be a tune that he really liked, and it's as though . . . I mean, it's a coincidence. It must be. But somehow I feel that that's his way. If he was going to get in touch with me it would be through music. (Mrs. N [widowed thirteen years], transcript, 23)

- [*Interviewer:* Do you ever feel the presence of your husband?]
  Oh yes! Very often! Very often. Because sometimes I'll sit in here and somebody'll say, "Mary!" and I'll look round, and I thought, "Well, I've not done it! I've not said that!" you know. Yeah, I have, about three times. Yes, I can honestly say that. About three times . . . and somebody said, "Mary!" and I've thought, "That's Tom!" you know. Because I know there's nobody else it could be. But that has happened three times. (Mrs. Q [widowed three years], transcript, 21)

Later Mrs. Q adds, "You know— and I mean, I'd like to—I like to know he's still here with us. Some people think it's perhaps a bit silly, but, no, I don't" (transcript, 24).

- [*Interviewer:* So do you ever feel the presence of your husband?]

  I did at first, yes, and I still talk— His photograph's behind the [?] by the way, behind the card. Yes, I still talk to him, odd times. If things are not going right. . . . Yeah, I do feel his presence, and this is why, when my daughter-in-law wanted me to get rid of that china cabinet I refused. Because we worked damned hard to get that when we were first married, and I've got so many little knickknacks, as you can see. It's full of mementoes and I will not throw them away, you know—

  [*Interviewer:* OK. You said that you feel the presence of your husband, used to feel it. More strongly at first?]

  Yeah, strongly at first. Very strong.

  [*Interviewer:* I mean, what form did it take?]

  Well, I was going to say this. I mean, it sounds a little bit far-fetched. He used to rub hisself, when he'd got aches or pains, with a certain rub, and it had got like a smell with it. It was one of these in a tube. I can't think of it now. . . . And I was going to say, I know I once went into the bedroom afterwards, one night I think it was, and the smell was there, and yet there was none of it left in the house, you know, and I just couldn't explain it. But, as I say, it was there.

  [*Interviewer:* OK. Did that use to happen at any particular point or—?]

  No, no. But his presence— I still feel as though, as I say, that he's here. Because, as I say, it was only, what?, about a fortnight ago that I paid my mortgage off, and I went and got the deeds, and my friend, the one I was telling you about, went with me, and she said to me, "He's looking down on you, you know, and he's very proud." . . . But, no. I do feel his presence a bit. (Mrs. R [widowed twenty years], transcript, 11–12)

- [*Interviewer:* Do you still talk to him now?]
  Oh yes, but in a different sort of way really because I can't lumber you with the fact that [?] two or three times I know he's been there—
  [*Interviewer:* Is there any particular circumstance? How do you know he's there?]
  Because I've not dreamt it. I've told my daughter so. Where I've known, the last time he was, I woke up. I know on and off I was awake. I wasn't dreaming, and I woke up and I could feel him at the side of me. I know you might not think it's— But you could see because we used to lie like that, back to back you know, and I know I was awake because it had happened before and funnily enough, it's gone [?] and I lie there and I think to myself, "Yes, I can feel him there." I'm saying this to myself, not out loud, and I say, "I'm not going to move because he'll go away." So I wasn't asleep, was I? No. I wasn't! I know I wasn't! and I just lie there. I could just— He wasn't moving, but I could feel him. You would know someone was there. Yes, yes, yes, and after a bit, I don't know whether I moved or what happened, but he went away. But this has happened to me two or three times— (Mrs. S [widowed fifteen years], transcript, 13)

- [*Interviewer:* Do you still feel that presence of your husband?]
  Oh, yes [indistinguishable]. Because if you look at the son, you start looking at your husband. . . . [Son] used to say all his actions were just his dad's. (Mrs. T [widowed six years], transcript, 6–7)

- *First widow (group interview):* Can I tell you an experience? This sounds unnatural, but it happened. Because I told you how I was, but we did sleep together for a long time, but we slept separate for five years. But this particular night, he'd only been dead about three or four weeks and I was in bed and asleep (well, I must have been half awake and half asleep) and this is honestly true. It's not imagination. I felt a warm— warmth all going down my back, and I laid like that and it was just as though somebody was in, it needn't have been a man, it could have been anybody. I had this warmth as though somebody was laying at the back of me for a long, long time, and I laid in bed like that and I thought— Then I woke up. I laid like that and I looked round and I thought, "Oh, there's somebody come upstairs and they've got into bed with me!" and this is true! "They've got in bed with me." This warmth was so intense, and I thought (I know it's daft now I'm looking back at it) I thought a burglar had got upstairs and laid in—. Well, you do read these things! And I laid there I don't know how long, a good ten minutes, and I dare not move, and I was just like that, holding my stomach like that, and I thought, "Oooh!" and I started to cry, and after a while something made me turn over, and to that day I don't know what it was. But I wondered if I'd been dreaming about Jack and this— they do talk about spirits, I don't know— and I don't know. It sounds like an imaginative thing but it really, really happened. God's truth. I'm not just saying it to make you think, "Ooh, you know, she had to be different!" It really, really happened! (transcript, 34–35).

Second widow (group interview): I really saw my husband now, about six or seven weeks after. I'd gone to sleep. I'd had a sleeping tablet. I couldn't sleep, and I woke up to hear somebody say, "Lucy, Lucy, Lucy," and I woke up, and it was like I am now, and just inside the bedroom door was John, HONESTLY! and he gave me the loveliest smile, and he'd got his lovely silver-grey suit on, and that was it. Never dreamt about him since or anything. But it was real. It was really real (transcript, 35).

So, among the Leicester widows the experience of "sensing the presence" of their husbands has been common and, as far as one can tell, it is not restricted to any one particular period of the bereavement. Two widows say they felt it in the early stages, and at the one-year mark, and they still feel it now. Two more felt it at the beginning and still feel it now; two mention that they felt it in the early weeks and months; five others say they feel it now. The experience has ranged from "seeing" the father in the son, through the classic ineffable "feeling" that he is there, through clear sensory experiences, to the "messages" of mediums. Hearing the voice of the lost husband giving advice or making comments on changes around the house are perhaps the most common experiences reported; others may smell an odor particularly associated with their husband, or may see him. It is not clear whether Mrs. I literally "sees" her dead husband on the patio or pictures him there, but the second widow who speaks in the group interview certainly sees her husband quite clearly. The sense of touch is also involved surprisingly often: two, possibly three, women have felt that he is in bed with them. Only one of these accounts (that of the first widow in the group interview) is frightening.[12]

We would suggest that there is a clear continuum in these narratives. The experiences stretch from Mrs. N's vague suppositions through to the second widow's distinct sensory experiences. Some correspond very closely to the Manchester stories told by Clara and Laura that began this chapter. Thus they further connect to the story Violet tells about her mother as "witness" in chapter 2, and beyond that to Alma's full-blown visitation. We seem to be dealing with types of experience that are very common among bereaved people, which can be elaborated into public stories, and which tradition has explanations for.

Clearly these are experiences that call out for interpretation. Though the Leicester question was invariably phrased in neutral language ("Do you ever feel your husband's presence?" "Did you feel he was still around?" and so on), nevertheless most of the Leicester widows developed their answers in a way that showed they had an implicit interpretive framework for understanding their experiences. There are, as we have seen, two dominant frameworks available for interpretation, the traditions of belief and disbelief discussed earlier. The rationalist "tradition of disbelief" is well-exemplified in the psychological literature with its language of "illusion," "hallucination," and "dissociative states."[13]

Here, the happenings are interpreted as symptoms or side effects of stress, broken hearts, and minds in chaos, or as part of the futile "searching" for the deceased that characterizes the early stages of grief. Only one of the Leicester widows, however, unequivocally adopts this approach to her own experience: "It's all in the mind," says Mrs. M about her feeling that her husband is in bed with her.

The other ready-made interpretive tradition is the supernaturalist one, the "tradition of belief." Among the Leicester widows there is one woman who has plainly opted into this tradition in its spiritualistic form with its language of "souls" and "spirits" and "passing over" (a form, of course, from which the Manchester women would distance themselves). Mrs. D consults a medium and attends the spiritualist church: "I know he's around," she says, "because, as I say, since I've been interested in the spiritual side, you— they [the mediums] give you messages." Her friend, Mrs. S, has also attended seances. She explains:

- . . . and I have been to— my friend and I have been— to these, what do you call them?
  [*Interviewer:* Spiritualist churches?]
  No, well, not to the church.
  [*Interviewer:* Oh yes, I know, where they have a medium. Yeah.]
  I went to the Church once, but nothing happened. I was hoping they were going to say something to me but never did. But— I've been to a couple of mediums on my own, privately like. But, not for many years, not recently. But, as I say, occasionally, I know he's there, you know, maybe not all the time, but—
  [*Interviewer:* Have you felt his presence recently or is that something that was—?]
  This was quite recently the last time. Yes, it's, it's not a year ago. Months ago, probably.
  [*Interviewer:* So does that happen at any particular point or—?]
  No, I wish I— I wish I knew [laughs] I could sort of— I could sort of conjure it up [still laughing]. You know, sometimes I just talk to him, you know, and if I'm a bit

upset. I was really upset about something, I can't remember what it was now. Oh, you do get times when you get so depressed, you know. You know, and— my daughter . . . wasn't very well at all these few months ago, and I was very, very down thinking she was ill and, oh you know, feeling sorry for myself, and I think then, that's when it happened, when he came, like, to the side of me.

Though Mrs. S refers to mediums and seances, what her account most strongly recalls are the "witness" beliefs that were discussed in the previous chapter—the informal, noninstitutionalized aspect of the various "traditions of belief" available through the folklore network. Other answers also suggest at least emergent or latent interpretations on the same lines ("and it's surprising, they do [help one]," says Mrs. C; "Just looking after us, I think," says Mrs. J).

Others at least interpret their experience as "real" rather than illusory ("but, yes, he does come back," says Mrs. I; "I like to know he's still here with us," says Mrs. Q). The first widow to speak in the group interview tries to account for her experience first in terms of "burglars" and then in terms of "spirits" but does not describe it as a "hallucination." Two others also use language that clearly implies belief in their experiences as "real" rather than illusory: Mrs. A frames her response in terms of her usual skepticism and the "strangeness," in this context, of her experiences; the second widow to speak in the group interview concludes, "But it was real. It was really real." Mrs. N uses both the rationalist and supernaturalist frameworks to try to account for her feelings: "and it's as though— I mean, it's a coincidence. It must be. But somehow I feel that that's his way, if he was going to get in touch with me it would be through music." Most of the Leicester widows therefore seem to have found that traditions of belief fit their experience as well as, or better than, traditions of disbelief.

Conclusion

The Leicester data are in tune with the earlier findings from the Manchester study, and help to contextualize the traditions of belief discussed above within the experiences of bereavement. It seems to us that a clear continuum exists between the "sense of presence" that is a recognized and ubiquitous feature of grieving and the accounts of the activities of "witnesses." Having said this, we want to stress that ours is not a reductionist agenda. We are very far from arguing that experiences of witnesses are disordered imaginings of the newly bereaved. All we are saying is that the sense of presence—a common feature of bereavement—is capable of being interpreted in different ways according to different intellectual traditions, one of which is the witness tradition. Nor are we suggesting that the witness tradition itself is "just folklore" in the sense of a false belief, an old wives' tale. The supernaturalist culture, which accredits these experiences to contact with the dead, is just as elegant and economical as the rationalist culture, which discounts this explanation, and much more satisfying.

Whatever the origin of these experiences, they are very "real," and of considerable interest to scientists as well as folklorists. Carl Jung was undoubtedly right when he wrote:

> There are universal reports of these post-mortem phenomena. . . . They are based in the main on psychic facts which cannot be dismissed out of hand. Very often the fear of superstition, which strangely enough, is the concomitant of universal enlightenment, is responsible for the hasty suppression of extremely interesting reports which are then lost to science. (Jung 1964, 316)

What also seems clear is that witness experiences (and perhaps many other similar "supernatural" experiences) should be studied within the context of the lasting sorrow of bereavement. This, in turn, entails that models of bereavement should be updated to recognize that "lasting sorrow" is a normal and frequent outcome of the death of someone who was important in one's life. The Leicester interviews seem to indicate that a measure of grief often persists for a very long time. It may become muted, buried, or healed over, but for many people it does not entirely go away. Those of us who have suffered a deep loss must find ourselves chilled by Erich Lindemann's words when he states that successful "grief work" will end in "emancipation from the bondage to the deceased" (1944, 143). Grievers do not consider their love to be bondage nor feel that they need to be "emancipated." As Mrs. C says: "You can't spend years with someone and then just cast them aside" (transcript, 12). Indeed, in private and after having suffered several painful bereavements himself, even Freud seems to have recognized the impossibility of abandoning dearly loved people just because they are dead. In a letter of 1929, he wrote:

> Although we know that after such a loss the acute stage of mourning will subside, we also know that we will remain inconsolable and will never find a substitute. No matter what may fill the gap . . . it nevertheless remains something else. And actually, this is how it should be; it is the only way of perpetuating that love which we do not want to relinquish. (quoted in Sanders 1989, 26)

We believe that many current models of bereavement which medicalize grief project a somewhat distorted picture, especially in that they are underpinned by analogies to physical trauma from which the successful and expected outcome is a full recovery. Furthermore, social adjustment, ability to manage one's own affairs, and independence of state welfare services, family, and friends may be good things in themselves, but they do not represent "recovery" from grief.

We believe that both the sense of presence and "witness" experiences grow out of the lasting bonds of love between two people, which death does not entirely sever. The metaphor so poignantly used in "No Road," Philip Larkin's poem of parting, is very relevant here. Larkin imagines the decision of two lovers to part in terms of neighbors who have decided to block the road that runs between their properties. As yet, their neglect has had little effect and the road is still passable:

> Leaves drift unswept, perhaps; grass creeps unmown;
> No other change.
> So clear it stands, so little overgrown,

> Walking that way tonight would not seem strange,
> And still would be allowed . . .

In time, however, their separation will draft "a world where no such road will run/From you to me." That is the culmination of their will but also what ails them.

Larkin was, of course, writing about a voluntary separation. Where the parting is forced and not willed, the road stays open a long time, and many do walk that way.

Chapter 4

From Private Experience to Public Performance

Supernatural Experience as Narrative

THE WOMEN WHOSE STORIES APPEAR IN THIS BOOK RELIED VERY extensively on narratives to put over their point of view and evaluate their experiences. The framework of the Leicester study was overtly narrative, but the women in the Manchester study were never directly asked to tell a story. They were simply invited to express an opinion about serious issues such as life after death, contacts between the living and the dead, the possibility of receiving forewarnings of critical life events, and so on. Nevertheless, they did tell stories—208 altogether, 150 of which were strictly relevant to the subjects under discussion (7 were local rumors about haunted houses; 143 were memorates).

Memorates directly rise out of this sort of context. For most people, experience is the best evidence for any belief (see, for example, Butler 1990, 99; Dégh and Vázsonyi 1974, 231; Glassie 1982, 69; Mullen 1978, 26). In the Manchester study, it was rare for women to express an opinion without adding some sort of explanatory or justificatory gloss. Of a total of 551 answers to direct questions, only 135 were an unelaborated "yes," "no," or "don't know"; in the other 416 cases the women made at least a minimal effort to show that they had a good reason for holding the opinion they did and that they were aware of the issues involved. Such explanations and justifications came in two overall forms. A minority of respondents appealed to reason or principle in such arguments as "God wouldn't allow it" or "It was Saint Paul, wasn't it, said we're encompassed with a great cloud of witnesses?" However, in over two-thirds of cases answers were glossed with an appeal to experience. In some cases these were brief statements such as "I've read about that" or "Well, I've experienced it," but more typically answers to questions were made up of a brief assent, followed by a short explanation and then an illustrative story. Alternatively, the speaker launched straight into narrative. So, when asked about whether they believed the dead can return to this world, for example, informants replied:

- Oh yes, yes, yes. Oh, yes. I do, yes. And again! I have PROOF of that! My grandmother. . . . (Margot)

- My little boy was drowned in the brook. Did you not know? Well, I can tell you about that. I can tell you what happened with that. . . . (Laura)

- I do. I do believe, but my family don't. But I'll give you an idea. . . . (Winifred)

- I think I must be a little bit psychic. I had one rather strange experience. . . . (Maura)

- Isn't it extraordinary that? And I remember once. . . . (Elisabeth)

- Yes, well, ACTUALLY, a long time ago. . . . (Kate)

- Yes! You see, my mother died when I was very small, and. . . . (Dora)

Just as one would expect, given the ways that belief in the supernatural is traditionally justified, even women whose preferred discourse mode seemed to be abstract rather than empirical tended to add experiential glosses to affirmative answers.

If extended or elaborated, these experiential glosses may become stories. The speaker may, for example, directly reply to a question, "Yes, I do," follow up with, "Well, so many people have experienced it," and then begin to discuss these experiences. When she judges that she has prepared the ground enough, she changes tempo and intonation, shifts to the past tense, and creates an opening for a story by refocusing from the general to the particular.[1] When she has told her story, or as much of it as she wants, she wraps it up by shifting back to the present tense again, evaluating the events or reporting on the current state of affairs.[2] She may, however, continue to discuss the subject in general terms until another topic arises. So memorates grow out of discussion and fade back into it.

The analysis in this chapter is based on the assumption that the content of a story is not the only, or even the most, important thing about it. As several commentators have pointed out, it should not be assumed that a story is simply an event "translated" into words (see, for example, Cohan and Shires 1988, 21). Indeed, in some cases, the telling *is* the story. I also assume that *uncovering* the ways of telling *discovers* the ways of meaning (as Dell Hymes has observed, "the structure is intrinsic to what . . . there is felt to be of . . . meaning" in many stories [1981, 62]), and also that the way a storyteller presents a narrative to a listener and together they negotiate the details are both crucial to the "point" that finally emerges (Polyani 1979).

Much work in personal narrative recently has been aimed at showing how narrators construct identities for themselves (see, for example, Roemer 1992; Workman 1992). The aim here is to pursue an even more elusive quarry—to try to discover how narrators invite listeners to construct meanings from raw events. Before we begin, however, I want to make a brief digression in order to point out that we can never be too confident, too absolute, in any judgment about oral storytelling. Everything is a matter of more-or-less, rather than all-or-nothing. As Keith Cunningham has trenchantly noted, "people will tell stories as they damn well please" (1979, 48). There are poor storytellers as well as good ones; there are reluctant and bashful narrators, narrators who change their minds about the point of a story halfway through telling it, and narrators who dry up for no discernible reason before they get to the end. And, of course, stories, especially memorates, are influenced by their immediate context in many indefinable, and usually unnoticed, ways. The hearer, too, is an essential part of that context—to the speaker, he or she is perhaps the most important part, whose reactions, gestures, gaze, and facial expressions will not only be constantly monitored but constantly reacted to. A speaker may abandon a story simply because the listener has glanced at her hands.

With these provisos in mind, remembering that there will be many exceptions to the patterns outlined and that my intent is not to lay down rules but only to describe what I have myself observed, I want to move on to considering how narrators build and perform memorates when they are "discourses" (see below, pages 124–37), told in order to explain, justify, or illustrate points of view.

BELIEF AND DISBELIEF: PATTERNS OF NARRATION

Let us begin by looking at two stories in the context of the interview conversations. The first story is told by Joan, a married woman in her seventies. I have asked her about "THINGS in houses." She explains that she is selling her house and made an appointment for a young couple to view it:

- They came the other night with this little boy and he was about four, they said he was about four, and took this child round with them, and they got as far as the spare room, and he hadn't said much at all.

  But apparently he liked the cellar (he thought that was terrific!) and the other rooms, and then they went up to the room at the top which we've always called the attic . . . and the child came down, sat in the corner for a minute, and then he told this most FANTASTIC story about there being a GHOST up there.

  I said, "A ghost?" I said, "Well, that's very odd. I've never seen a ghost and I've lived here a VERY long time." I said, "I've never seen one. I'd LOVE to see one. What's he LIKE?" you see. So—

  "Oh, he's a nasty one, a nasty one."

  So his father said, "Well, there's NICE ghosts as well as nasty ones."

  "Oh, this was a NASTY one, Daddy."

  So I said, "Well, what did he LOOK like?"

  "Oh, I didn't SEE him," he said. "I HEARD him. He was talking to another ghost, and he was nasty too!"

The second story was told by Vera, a single woman in her sixties, when the subject of discussion turned to the value of religious faith:

- Different instances in my life I feel that I've been guided or helped—
  [G. B.: Do you? Can you recall any of them in particular?]
  Well— just— worried about certain things and then they all come right in a way that I'd have never foreseen, if I just— just have faith and trust. I don't trust a lot, that's my trouble. But— I've had a really, a very happy life. My "lines have fallen in pleasant places" always.
  My mother was Highland and she was a— Well, once or twice I see her come back, and she comes if there's anything— ILL going to happen in my family, anything like that.
  [G. B.: Really?]
  Yes.
  [G. B.: Really.]
  Any trouble or anything. Before my brother-in-law died— that was about the last incident that happened in my family, he— she came. I could see her, you know, quite distinctly and I said, "Well, something's happened. Something's going to happen," and I heard just a day or two after that George had died suddenly— and— any trouble in the family— she's there, she's always come, but I feel that she's there,—
  [G. B.: Yes, you actually—]
  and not very far away. I don't know—
  [G. B.: Isn't that strange?]
  Isn't it?

On the face of it, Joan's story is "better" than Vera's—it is brisk, neat, rounded, and chronological, whereas, in comparison, Vera's seems confused and lacking point or resolution. Joan's also takes an unambiguous linear form, moving from scene-setting to event to resolution, and ending with a humorous punch line. Vera's story, on the other hand, is a repetitious accumulation of more or less specific examples of representative experiences. After a long preamble and a false start ("My mother was Highland and she was a—"), she begins as if she is about to tell a story then fades into generalizations ("Well, once or twice I see her come back, and she comes if there's anything— ILL going to happen in my family"). She then refocuses in terms of a specific example ("Before my brother-in-law died"), and finally ends with another generalized statement which adds a bit of detail missed from the other renditions ("I feel that she's there— and not very far away.") Vera is not moving the narrative on in brisk chronological sequence, she is circling round a central point.

In the context of discussion, however, Joan's story is actually less helpful than Vera's. Her initial reply to my question is brief and noncommittal, then she tells her little narrative, ending with its humorously delivered punch line. Though there may be something odd about her attic, the story shows, she is too wise to treat the traditional explanation as anything more than a joke. After Joan's story the subject is closed. Unless the hearer is very brave, she cannot discuss it or use it to explain her own ideas.

On the other hand, in the context of a problem-solving discussion, Vera's narrative shows itself to be both properly structured and effectively performed. Whereas Joan's story prevents discussion, Vera's invites it. Her story arises out of a conversation about religious faith and is meant to illustrate her theme. It is subjective and personal. Traditional beliefs in the power of the dead to operate in the mundane world are fully incorporated into her thought patterns. The story is part of a reasoned discourse. Afterwards, the subject continues. I ask her whether she actually sees her mother (Vera answers that her mother is "like a grey shadow") and we discuss whether other relatives may come back to warn their descendants, and so on. This is the natural response to the story, not just the reaction of a folklorist interested in supernatural traditions.

The performative styles (less obvious on the printed page) are fitted to the aims of the narrators and the effect they wish to produce on their audience. For instance, the tape recordings show quite distinct intonations and voice quality between the two speakers. Joan uses a lively, vivacious voice, a great deal of stress, varied tempo, strategic pauses, and chuckles of amusement. She is providing an entertainment. Vera's voice, on the other hand, is low, her tempo slow, her intonation almost monotonous, even her bit of dialogue is hardly differentiated from the surrounding discourse. There is a sad, reflective quality to it. She is plainly thinking out loud.

These two stories are admirable illustrations of linguist Émile Benveniste's distinction between stories told as history and stories told as discourse. When a narrator calls attention to the recounting of events, is aware of the audience and intends to influence them in some way, Benveniste says, the story is "discourse"; when, on the other hand, "events that took place in a moment of time are presented without any intervention of the speaker" the story is a "history" (quoted in Cohan and Shires 1988, 92–94).

Another way of conceptualizing the difference might be to think of Joan's story as "action-description" (van Dijk 1974–75) and Vera's as "exposition" (Longacre 1976, 200–202). In the context of a serious discussion of beliefs, "histories" and "action-descriptions" are inappropriate because they are rounded, finished. Though a storyteller cannot actually prevent audience participation, the finality of these sorts of stories does inhibit it; the audience is left with nothing much to do except admire the effect. In my experience, if a speaker offers "action-descriptions" in the context of discussions of belief it usually signals his or her wish not to engage in debate; where speakers are in tune with their hearer and happy with the subject matter, they are more likely to adopt alternative performative strategies geared to the exploration of belief and opinion. This is the pattern throughout all the Manchester material. Of forty stories structured (like Joan's) in a neat linear sequence, only seven were told by women with a positive or open-minded attitude toward traditional beliefs. With the exception of these seven, speakers who were willing or anxious to talk consistently interleaved their observations with stories (like Vera's) in which the sequence of time and event was less simply and naturalistically presented.

The discursive nature of stories told in this sort of context is admirably illustrated in the extended passage below, where we see a memorate growing out of a discussion and fading back into it.

The speaker is Violet, a married woman in her sixties. She has been telling me how she senses her mother's presence. I remark that this is "very common with ladies," and this encourages her to firm up her presentation; when she takes up the threads of her theme again, it is in a more explicit mode. Then she abruptly changes tense to the past and introduces a specific example, thus making an aperture for her story. The narrative that follows is told in almost circular fashion. Violet reiterates her belief in her mother's "nearness," then drops back into the abstract mode using the present tense. Finally, she draws an appropriate conclusion hinting at a religious interpretation, which could be used to lead into a different, but related, conversation:

- But I always feel the nearness of my mother, always, but not my father. It's my mother I feel that's near.
  [G. B.: I think it seems to be sort of very common with ladies. They feel that their mother is with them afterwards.]
  That's right, yes—
  [G. B.: And, as you say, not the fathers.]
  My mother—
  [G. B.: Some of them have even seen their mothers or heard their voices.]
  Yes. I've never, you know, actually could say I've heard her voice but I've felt that she's kind of "Well, I'm here with you, you know, and I'll help you!"
  Now, for instance. My brother died suddenly and he had a bungalow in North Wales and we had to get rid of it, Howard and I, in—
  Now, it seems incredible that we could clear that bungalow, a big bungalow, and sell it for cash in one week, but we didn't do that on our OWN, you know, you COULDN'T! Not— When I look back, I couldn't have done it off my own STEAM! I had HELP there!
  You know, we both look back and we think, "Well! We never could have done it off our own steam!" It was sold for cash, you know, and all the furniture went. We cleared it in a week. You know, it's incredible really, and

I FELT then as if I was being shown what to do. Because I'm a poor one at making decisions and this is where I've always leant to my mother, and I feel she's the ONE that PUSHES me to know what to do.
[G. B.: One of my friend's mothers told me something very much like this.]
Oh, yes, I believe— I do really quite believe— that you do get help. I believe my mother is still around me and, I mean, I'm not being dramatic or anything. I've always felt this. I've always said this to my husband that I've always felt my mother quite close to me. Because she was a good mother, a good-living— and had to work hard.

The nature of this discourse is plainly expository. Like the abstract description it is embedded in, the story itself, when it comes, is task-related. It is designed to explicate a complex viewpoint by embodying it in a personal example. Moreover, it is by means of the story that she clarifies her exact position on the most controversial aspect of the discussion—that is, whether the souls of the dead can manifest themselves physically or only spiritually. It is the story, too, that is likely to be taken up by the hearer and used to discuss the problem, and which will do most to convince a skeptical hearer of the plausibility of her ideas. The way the story is presented to the listener is therefore crucially important to the success of the whole discourse. It is as vital that it should function efficiently as explanation as that it should engage interest as narrative.

These constraints necessarily color the way the story is structured and performed. It acquires its typical characteristics because the narrator has an inner need to describe events truthfully, remember them accurately, and interpret them meaningfully. She also has a social need to have her definition of the experience confirmed in order that her view of reality may be sanctioned. The force of the story is therefore at once expository and heuristic. Such stories are not only told in the *context* of discussions of belief, they *are* discussions of belief. Through them, the speaker is seeking clarification of the meaning of the episode (Robinson 1981, 69), and striving "to reach conclusions from premises" (Dégh and Vázsonyi 1973, 299).

In the section that follows I want to explore in more detail some storytelling strategies geared to decision-making in matters of belief.

Story Dialectic: The Imaginary Judge and Jury

The names of Linda Dégh and her late husband, Andrew Vázsonyi, are intimately associated with the study of narrative, especially the discourse of legends. I believe their most important contribution is the concept of legends as debates about belief. This idea has been put forward in a stream of insightful publications, but especially in their influential monograph *The Dialectics of Legend* (1973). As they see it, legends document the sudden collision of two worlds (the mundane and the extraordinary or supernatural) that ought to be kept distinct. The essence of legend-performance is therefore some form of debate. The storyteller may be supported and encouraged by the listener, who may help to round up the details of the story and negotiate a sympathetic interpretation of the events; on the other hand, he or she may be challenged, contradicted, and forced to engage in a verbal duel with the listener.

I agree with these observations, but I want to make two caveats. First, I want to point out that these features may be characteristics of any story with problematic contents when told in a face-to-face context and when the discursive force is interpretational or heuristic. It is not necessary to define every story which features this sort of debate as a "legend." Secondly, I want to note that most of the work on the "dialectics of legend" (or, as I would prefer to term it, "story dialectic") has focused on debates between speakers and hearers; yet another sort of debate is possible. As Dégh and Vázsonyi note: "the dispute takes place on several levels and on different fronts in which the . . . teller discusses his belief *with himself*, but mostly with a real or *imaginary audience*" (Dégh and Vázsonyi 1973, 5; my emphasis). I believe that debates where the speaker argues with him- or herself or with an imaginary audience (which I think of as "internal dialectic") is as much a part of heuristic storytelling as that between a narrator and a real audience. In my experience, internal dialectic is an especially common feature of memorate-telling. Those who bring their private experience into the public domain by presenting it as a story in defense of traditions of belief are acutely aware that their audience may interrupt or challenge them using the familiar arguments drawn from the rationalist world view. So they tell the story in ways designed to prevent this happening. If they anticipate an adversarial response, they try to disarm the expected criticisms before they are uttered. Though the story is full of debate, the speaker conducts much of that discussion alone, debating with him- or herself about the meaning and nature of the events, thus at least temporarily holding off any outside challenge.

Internal dialectic may take many forms: in the paragraphs below I sketch in four of the more obvious ones. The first two I discuss have been mentioned in Dégh's work; the third and fourth have not, as far as I am aware. I have myself drawn attention to them in an earlier paper, though not as dialectical features in the Déghian sense (Bennett 1986). Here, I take the opportunity to bring them under the umbrella of this attractive concept, where I think they properly belong.

The Accusing I

Here is a story told by Edie, a seventy-year-old widow, which shows a storyteller obviously engaging in a debate with herself. She is presenting the arguments for both the supernaturalist and the rationalist interpretations in order to arrive at a decision about the meaning of the events. I have italicized the internal dialectical elements for the sake of clarity:

- Shall I tell you why I have this belief as well, which sounds really— *I mean, you'll think, "Did she see it, or didn't she?"*

  It's the one thing that happened in my life when my father died.

  We went to the funeral and it was in town. We went to the funeral (Mother lives at Brighton on the south coast) and the funeral was over and everything, and we were sort of coming back and Aunty's staying with Mother (you know how you do all these arrangements?)

and I went in to look at my father's bedroom before I came away.

I just went and had a look, both the bedrooms. I just wanted to look, you know, and I just stood there looking and I SAW three whiffs of smoke.

D'you KNOW that? You know, like a CIGARETTE!

Well, I smoke, but I wasn't smoking then. I'm sure I DID! (you know what I MEAN?) and my father was a very heavy smoker, you know. It sounds crazy, this.

Now, all right. I could be wrong about that. Somebody else could have looked in the bedroom and had a cigarette before I went in.

But I honestly DID! About three RINGS, something like THAT [demonstrates]. Isn't it ODD, that?

Now, the only thing I've sort of satisfied myself was, "Oh yes. Somebody else has been upstairs and they've been in there and had a cigarette."

But they were THERE!

One can see at a glance how the primary force of the story is an attempt at evaluating the experience. Edie is acutely aware of the possibility of being challenged. She not only constantly appeals for confirmation, she is also sensitive to the way her listener might respond ("I mean, you'll think, 'Did she see it, or didn't she?'"). In addition, just at the crucial moment when a straightforward tale would build up to a denouement, Edie's story drifts away into speculation in which assertion ("Well, I smoke, but I wasn't smoking then") is balanced against counter-assertion ("Somebody else could have looked in the bedroom and had a cigarette before I went in"). What is going on here is a debate between the supernaturalist and rationalist world views, though there is but a single voice—Edie's own—to express both the believer's case and the skeptic's challenge.

In another story, told by Gloria*, a middle-aged married woman, the internal dialectic is aimed at an imaginary critic:

- Only ONE time that I VIVIDLY remember, and this was many years ago, and we were in SPAIN, and my husband's mother— we WANTED to take her with us, actually, but she wouldn't come, and— Ooh, this must be about eight years ago, and this was about— two o'clock in the morning.

Now, it wasn't dark or anything. We'd just come back from a nightclub (yes, I think it was in 1971, when it was very cheap), and my husband was in the bathroom— he was cleaning his teeth or something[3]— and I just said to him (and we'd not had a lot to drink or anything like that), I said, "It's funny. I've just seen your mam. Isn't it silly?"

Now, all the lights were on, and I forgot ALL about it until the next morning.

We were going out to this bowling that they have in the open air, and we had a telegram saying that his mother had died.

That was unexpected, because, although she had sugar diabetes, when we left her about eight days previously she was well, and she died, as the coroner thinks, about quarter to two on the Tuesday night, but it was the Wednesday morning before they found out, because the bedroom door was LOCKED and they couldn't get in.

Now that— and I've never forgotten that.

It's very funny.

Gloria knows what she saw and, though she never says so, it is plain that she interprets it in traditional terms as a visitation from her mother-in-law at the moment of death. However, she is very aware of the arguments that rationalists will put forward to destroy her case. She is also sensitive to the social criticism her story might attract. Each of these potential challenges is met and answered in the details of the story. Set against each other in tabular form, anticipated challenges and implicit answers become clearer:

Gloria is able to build up an unshakable case because of the debate with her imaginary critic. It is a good piece of storytelling anyway, but the internal dialectic makes it a good piece of analysis too.

potential social challenge	*answer*
1. "How wicked of you to go off on holiday leaving your sick mother-in-law alone . . ."	"we WANTED to take her with us, actually, but she wouldn't come" "although she had sugar diabetes, when we left her . . . she was well"
2. ". . . especially when you're spending money recklessly."	"it was in 1971, when it was very cheap"

potential philosophical challenge	*answer*
3. "If it was 2 A.M., then it would have been dark. What you saw must have been a shadow or something."	"it wasn't dark or anything" "all the lights were on"
4. "You were drunk and imagined it."	"we'd not had a lot to drink"
5. "You're just a silly woman."	"I've just seen your mam. Isn't it silly?" ["I know what you'll say, but . . ."]
6. "You were in some sort of abnormal state."	"my husband was in the bathroom cleaning his teeth" "we were going out to that bowling they have in the open air" ["we're just ordinary people doing ordinary things"]

Calling to Witness

"Legends are seldom limited to the mere relation of the plot," Dégh and Vázsonyi say, and

> In most cases the narrative itself cannot be separated from the circumstances of telling, the introductory remarks . . . interjected comments, and reflections of both teller and participants that parallel the performance

to the end. Furthermore, the closing remarks, explanatory, supplementary, or contrasting stories, analogous cases, and modifications, or straight refutation . . . are also inseparable parts of the legend. (1971, 287)

This feature is a constant in all the stories I collected and has also been observed in other genres (Toolan 1988, 169–73; Butler 1990, 113–15). Though Dégh and Vázsonyi did not elaborate this idea or treat it as a form of dialectic, it seems to me that these structural features are dialectical in both force and intent.

As an illustration, let us return to Edie's story and look for the closure. After the story is apparently complete (though still unresolved) and Edie has summed up in the phrase "But they were THERE!" she tacks another seemingly different story on to her narrative:

- When my husband died—
  My daughter teaches ballet, or she did do, she does television work now, and it was a very high building, you know, and there was this stained glass window and she said she saw her father looking through this window!
  You see what I mean?— and she's not like that! She's quite, you know, having a good time in life and— You see what I mean?
  I suppose there's something in some things.

With the words "When my husband died," Edie creates another opening for a story, then goes straight into the action, pauses for some more internal dialectic ("and she's not like that! She's quite, you know, having a good time in life and—"). Finally she signals the end of the story by returning to the present. Though this second bit of narrative looks like an afterthought, as a rounded exploration of reasons for belief the first story is not complete without the daughter's experience. The reframing of the argument by the reporting of another person's experiences is actually integral. And Edie signals it as such: the story that begins with "Shall I tell you why I have this belief as well" does not really end until the question has been matched with an appropriate answer, "I suppose there's something in some things." When this closure finally comes, Edie draws a firmer conclusion than can be justified by her own inconclusive experience and tentative arguments alone. The daughter's story has therefore served the dialectical function of providing support for the believer's case. Whereas before there was only one voice (Edie's own) having to be both advocate and challenger, with the introduction of the daughter's testimony through the recounting of her experience, the number of voices arrayed to speak in defense of the believer's case has been doubled.

A similar dialectical strategy underlies another two-part story. Earlier we saw how Lettie, a sixty-year-old widow, told a story about her mother's death. In point of fact, the story did not end quite where it appeared to, with her mother's dying smile. a second mini-story—a part 2—was tacked on to double the interpretational value. The characteristics of this story—its dependence on both "the accusing I" and "calling to witness"—are most plainly seen when the story is set out in tabular form so that the way it is built up can be more easily identified:

Part 1

Well, I've never believed in it at all. My husband wouldn't believe in it all— no point in discussing it.	*dialectic* *rationalist opinion*
But I saw my father.	*story aperture*
My father was the first to die, and he died at three o'clock in the morning, and then, twelve months afterwards, Mother died at three in the afternoon.	*scene-setting*
Well, she died of cancer of the jaw, so, I mean, there was nothing to SMILE about.	*dialectical commentary* *(preempts rational* *interpretation of experience* *she is about to relate)*
But just before she died, I felt that whatever there was, EVER there was,	*event*

"Alas, Poor Ghost!"

Father had come to meet her.
Because she just sat up and she gave that SMILE.

Of course, I think they do sit up before they die.
      dialectical commentary
      (rational interpretation
      of mother sitting up)

But— and she sort of held her arms out
      event
and it was just that SPECIAL SMILE she always kept for him—
      (with
      dialectical subtext—
      "that SPECIAL SMILE")

[*pause*]

[G. B.: You think she actually saw him?]
      resolution
I do! Oh, yes!
      resolution confirmed

Part 2
[*takes the form of recounting a dialectical debate*]

We were discussing this last year,
      aperture

---

and we were away,
      scene-setting

---

and the people we got friendly with,
      rationalist attitude
he was like my husband, "Once you're dead,
you're dead," you see,

---

and she was like me, "We none of us
      believer's attitude
know what it IS. I mean, it's something
      extra voice
we shan't know till we DIE."
      brought in on believer's side
But she was like me.
She felt there WAS something,

---

and the man who owned the hotel
      third voice
(there was he and his wife)
      to back up supernaturalist view
he was a great believer in "there was something—
WHAT we didn't know."

But our two men, of course, they were great disbelievers.	*rationalist attitude summarized*
That is the only time.	*preliminary closure*
I've always felt there IS something, WHAT we do not know.	*believer's attitude summarized*
But I always felt that FATHER CAME TO MEET HER.	*event as evidence*
I always felt that.	*final closure*

Evidential Scene-Setting

Internal dialectic may take even subtler forms. Chief of these is to make the scene-setting carry evidential weight. The storyteller behaves as if she were a witness in a court of law, whose reliability will be assessed by the completeness and accuracy of her memory of the circumstances. So the story is "flooded" with scene-setting to deter challenges to the narrator's role of remembrancer and interpreter.

An extreme example can be found in a story told by Polly, a widow in her seventies, when I ask her whether she believes in premonitions of death. However the structure of this story is analyzed, scene settings will be found to constitute a major part of the total narration. It is a part—a crucial part—of the evidence being presented and also a part of the process of evaluating the meaning of the experience. In Polly's story the very banality of the events of the fatal day, remembered in such fine detail, is the proof she presents to back up her negative reply to my question about premonitions. Again, the story is set out in tabular form for easy reference:

No. I'll tell you why. This is when my husband died.	*story aperture*
I was at a coffee-morning next door to me. It was a beautiful day like this on the first of February, and he was very, very fond of gardening,	*scene-setting*

and he said, "It's a gorgeous morning.
We could have a walk,"
but I couldn't.
We would have gone to the park.
We couldn't go to the park.
It was in the village, middle of the village.
So he said, "Never mind, dear. Don't bother.
The sun will be warmer this afternoon.
We'll go this afternoon.
We'll have an early lunch"—
we always had a sort of cold lunch—
"What are we having for lunch?"
So I said, "I tell you what,
we'll have some mushrooms," I said.
"Put them on at five minutes to one,"
and he said, "Right you are!"
I'm not saying we were sloppy or anything,
but we always kissed one another on the first of the month
and said, "Happy month!"
Not sort of silly, but we always had done.
He said, "Goodbye, dear, I hope it's a good morning."

At five to one, I looked at the clock   *event*
and said to the lady next door,
"I hope he's put those mushrooms on.
They should be very, very nice," you see,
and then I went back home
and there he was on the kitchen floor, dead,
and I had no premonition of that.

There are, perhaps, those who would say this simply shows how wordy and irrelevant women's storytelling is. But they would have missed the point. Though a naive observer might think that extensive scene-setting prevents the storyteller getting to the "point," in actual fact it *is* the point of the story; it is the dialectical focus.

Overlays

The same diagnostic and dialectical effect is sometimes achieved by replaying part or all of the story in accumulated layers of exposition.

The speaker refocuses, reiterates, or amplifies any story elements she chooses as often as she likes or in any way she likes, in a manner akin to the "overlays" described by J. E. Grimes in his study of non-European narrative (Grimes 1972; 1975, 292–97). Overlays present narrative information in overlapping planes, each of which backs up to some earlier time reference and starts over again, incorporating novel elements alongside the old ones, so the story accumulates subtleties and resonances of meaning as it unfolds. The story below shows this strategy being used to particularly good effect.

In the previous chapter, I quoted a story in which May, a married woman in her eighties, told about sensing the presence of her mother. This was the first of two versions, and was told to my father when I was out of the room. When I came back, she repeated it at rather longer length for my benefit. The version below is this second telling. Immediately after creating an aperture for her story and framing it as dialectic, May sets out on a prolonged scene-setting. Then she stops, refocuses, and begins again, creating another aperture and providing a second, much shorter, scene-setting that backtracks almost to where the story began. A third piece of scene-setting information brings the events forward to just before her mother's death. Then, in a single block of narrative with thirteen clauses but only two sentences, May recounts the central events and describes the nature of her experience of her mother's "presence." She then pauses for some rather defensive internal dialectic. Four more planes of event follow. The first three of these planes develop her discussion of the nature of the experience, successively focusing on the essential elements, and the last one briefly résumés them all. There is no resolution and no closure. May simply moves straight into post-narrative generalities. By using overlaid planes of narrative, she is able to keep returning to the contrast that is so important to her—that between the empty house and the bedroom full of her mother's presence. It is a superbly told story, both as narrative and as a heuristic exercise.

Before setting it out in tabular form to show the way the story twists and turns as May negotiates its meaning, it is worth making two observations. First, it is notable what good evidence it provides of the way the audience can affect the narrative performance and structure; and secondly, the fact that the version told to the unfamiliar person is the one with large amounts of scene-setting indicates that scene-setting is indeed, as I am suggesting, a dialectical tool.

Here is the story:

I don't know whether it was   *aperture 1*
my own imagination—   *frames the story as dialectic*

I'll say this before I start.   *scene-setting 1*
I was the only daughter   *general background*
and I had two brothers,
and my mother and I were rather close, very close,
and she lived with us
for seventeen years after my father died.
She was nearly ninety when she died
and she was only really seriously ill the last twelve months.
She had a stroke which left her memory impaired
but not her faculties.
She couldn't remember people and places.
She never remembered living in Newtown with me
before we came to Crofton,
but apart from that,
it was a case of when anyone came
she would say after they'd gone,
she covered up very well,
and then she would say,
"Tell me all about them and I would know next time."

But I was telling your father,   *aperture 2*

---

after she died, she died at home,   *scene-setting 2*
and she'd only been—   *briefly repeats earlier information*
She'd had a stroke, as I said,
and she was— she didn't wander at all.

And, anyway, then she had a second one   *scene-setting 3*
and she lived only a fortnight after that,   *shifts time-frame forward*
the last two days she was unconscious.

But after she died, I never felt she'd really gone.   *event 1*
Her presence seemed to be   *overview of experience*
particularly in her bedroom,

and it was about twelve months after
until her room felt empty to me,
and it was very strong at times, I would go up,
and I used to wake in the night
and think I heard her,
because she slept with her door open
and so did we, to hear her,
and I was confident I'd many a time heard her cough.

Well, that would be sheer imagination, of course.	*internal dialectic*

But it was the emptiness of the room,	*event 2*
and it was quite twelve months after,	*focuses on emptiness of room*
when we returned from the second holiday	
after she'd died,	
and then I realized that the room was empty.	

I've never expressed it before,	*commentary*

but it was there with me in whatever I was doing.	*event 3*
She was there somehow,	*focuses on presence*
either sitting watching me,	
or doing that.	

But suddenly the house was empty.	*event 4*
	recapitulates event 2

But I couldn't express it really.	*commentary*
It was just a feeling.	

I came back,	*event 5*
and before that I'd always felt	*recapitulates event 1*
that she was about somewhere,	
and it had gone.	

I suppose it does take twelve months	*post-narrative remarks*
to recover from things like that,	
I don't know, if you're close to anyone.	

Stories like these create an almost three-dimensional effect
through accumulation and accretion. They give narrators the best

possible chance of clarifying the significance of the events for themselves and their audiences. They are powerfully persuasive analytical tools—a way of privately thinking about, and publicly explaining, matters which are too difficult and too important to be dealt with in a linear story with its fast pace, chronological development, and slick resolution.

In Brief

The women who told the memorates I have discussed were not literary artists or professional tellers of tales. Nevertheless, they were effective storytellers. They not only communicated their experiences graphically, but they structured them so they could be used as "discussion documents" to negotiate world view and philosophy. The force of the stories was heuristic, the strategy strongly dialectical. The narratives grew out of experience, and the context of their telling was the discussion of tradition, experience, and belief.

Stories like this help to weld these important influences together into a coherent folklore that is a map of the interactions of the heavenly and mundane worlds.

Chapter 5

"Alas, Poor Ghost!"

Case Studies in the History of Ghosts and Visitations

As Pierre Le Loyer wrote in the sixteenth century, the supernatural "is the topic that people most readily discuss and on which they linger the longest because of the abundance of the examples, the subject being fine and pleasing and the discussion the least tedious that can be found" (quoted by John Dover Wilson in his introduction to Lavater [1572] 1929). All the stories so far have been oral ones told in the context of interviews and conversations and taken to be representative of the beliefs of many people living today.

However, popular folklore and beliefs have from time to time been taken up by men of letters, or by the religious or secular authorities, and used for their own purposes. No book about ghosts and visitations can be complete without at least glancing at these angles. However, an adequate history of supernatural belief in literature, religion, and politics would take an immense labour (even Keith Thomas's magisterial *Religion and the Decline of Magic* [1971] could only tackle developments over a limited period). So in this final chapter I claim to do no more than offer six snapshots that show individual moments in the flux of the intellectual traditions of writers and opinion leaders.

The Ghost of Hamlet's Father

One of the most famous apparitions in English literature is that which appears to Hamlet, Prince of Denmark, in Shakespeare's great tragedy, probably written at the turn of the sixteenth-seventeenth century. The date is a clue to Hamlet's ambivalence towards the ghost, and his tardiness to do its commands.

Hamlet was composed at the end of a century which had seen an almost constant struggle in England between Protestantism and Catholicism, Reformation and Counter Reformation, focused through the alternation of Protestant and Catholic monarchs. Henry VIII, who had signalled the breach with Rome in the early decades of the century, was followed in rapid succession by his children: the short-lived, ardently Protestant Edward VI; the Catholic zealot Mary, his daughter by Catherine of Aragon; then the Protestant Elizabeth I, his daughter by Anne Boleyn. During the whole of this period, the possibility of contact with the dead was a central issue in very serious and bitter religious disputes between Catholics and Protestants in Europe.

The Reformation in England initiated far-reaching attacks on church rituals, on the priesthood, and on all magical elements of religious doctrine. In particular, the doctrine of purgatory, which had served its turn for four hundred years or more, came under attack. Protestants argued that there was no such place: after the death of the body, the souls of the dead went straight to heaven or straight to hell according to their just deserts. No subsequent action on the part of survivors could help them thwart their destiny. Men and women were saved by the faith they had shown during their life, no amount of prayers, alms, masses, or indulgences could therefore save them after their death. To counter this argument, Catholic intellectuals called upon evidence from popular folklore about ghosts and visitations. History, tradition, experience, and the Bible, they argued, combined to vouch for the existence of ghosts—and where else could ghosts have returned from but purgatory? If, as the new Protestantism taught, the souls of the dead went straight to heaven or straight to hell, then there could be no such thing as ghosts because the blessed would not want to leave heaven and the damned would not be allowed to leave hell. But if ghosts existed, then so must purgatory. In Keith Thomas's words: "although it may be a relatively frivolous question today to ask whether or not one believes in ghosts, it was in the sixteenth century a shibboleth which distinguished Protestant

"Alas, Poor Ghost!"

from Catholic almost as effectively as belief in the Mass or Papal Supremacy" (1971, 598).

The Catholics' argument put Protestant divines into an awkward position. Argument demanded that they reject the notion of ghosts and apparitions in its entirety—to defeat the Catholic position it was necessary to discredit all known examples of ghostly visitations—yet this could not be easily done. Not only were there cases of ghostly apparitions in the Bible, most notably the appearance of the ghost of the prophet Samuel to King Saul under the mediumship of the Witch of Endor, but also there were centuries of popular tradition that spirits of the dead could indeed appear to men and women.

The Protestant answer to this dilemma was to discredit as much of the evidence as possible and redefine the remainder. In the writings of Lewes (Ludowig) Lavater we find the epitome of this approach. In discussing traditions of disbelief earlier, we saw how his *Of Ghosts and Spirits Walking by Night* (translated into English in 1572) was designed to prove that ghosts were not, and could not be, "the souls of dead men as some have thought." They were either the mistakes of silly, sick, or unduly sensitive people, or the result of deliberate deceit, or Catholic lies, or some natural thing misunderstood. The standard Protestant position was that most people were mistaken when they thought they saw a spirit. However, there was a possibility that Satan might disguise his devils in the shape of a dead person in order to wreak havoc with the lives and souls of poor mortals (Lea 1957, 65), and on rare occasions God might send an angel on a special mission.

A sophisticated reflection of Protestant thinking can be seen in *Doctor Faustus*, written by Shakespeare's contemporary Christopher Marlowe (d. 1593). When the devil Mephistopheles appears to Faustus, he insists that, despite appearances to the contrary, he is in hell even as he speaks with Faustus in his study. When Faustus asks, "How comes it then that thou art out of Hell?" Mephistopheles replies, "Why this is Hell, nor am I out of it," and goes on to explain that he carries his own hell of regret and deprivation around with him wherever he goes. What is not possible is that, having lost heaven, he can be anywhere else but hell. In contrast, the popular stereotypes of supernatural encounters on which

Catholic divines relied at the time may be seen in others of Shakespeare's plays. Banquo's gruesome ghost in *Macbeth* is one example, and the vengeful ghosts that bid Richard III despair on the eve of his crucial battle at Salisbury are another. These sorts of gaudy and terrifying apparitions, which appear to the person responsible for their death, were common motifs in the folklore of the day.

The ghost of Hamlet's father, however, is different from Banquo's ghost. He does not appear to those who have murdered him, but demands revenge from a third person. His demeanor is sober and, unlike Banquo, he is not tricked out in overt symbols of ghosthood, such as mangled wounds. These things—and the fact that other people can see him—all distance him somewhat from the popular tradition and make him a much more ambiguous figure.

As John Dover Wilson has noted: "much of the drama of the play's first act hinges on the uncertainty of the ghost's status" (Dover Wilson 1959, chap. 3). Where has he come from? Is he a force for good or evil? This is the dilemma that faces Hamlet. Horatio and the guards report no more than that they have seen a "figure *like* your father" (my emphasis). Their account makes the apparition *sound* like a traditional ghost: it walks at midnight in a liminal place and disappears at the first cockcrow; it appears to be anxious to make some sort of communication; it makes "the night hideous" by its presence; and it certainly looks like the king. But is it a ghost? And is it the king?

At first, Hamlet does not rush to judgment. He questions the guards very closely—"Where was this?" "Did you not speak to it?" "Arm'd, say you?" "Then saw you not his face?" "What, looked he frowningly?" "And fixed his eyes upon you?" "Stay'd it long?" "His beard was grizzled—no?" It is only when he has assured himself that the apparition does indeed appear to be the king that he decides to watch for it himself. Even so, he is plainly aware this might be risky. If it really is a ghost, it should pose no direct threat to him. If it is an angel disguised as an armed king, then it should be listened to because it is a sign that some dire trouble is brewing. But what if it is a devil pretending to be a ghost? He decides to take the risk of speaking to it: "If it assume my noble father's person/I'll speak to it, though Hell itself should gape/And bid me hold my peace," he says.

Here we see a direct consequence of the Protestant reclassification of ghosts into otherworldly messengers: it intensified the fracture of the supernatural realm into two opposed camps; and, more importantly, it left people unable to interpret their experiences—a "ghost" might be an angel or a demon, but there was no easy way of telling them apart. Hamlet certainly does not know what sort of spirit he is about to address: "Angels and ministers of grace defend us!/Be thou a spirit of health or goblin damned,/Bring with thee airs from Heaven or blasts from Hell/Be thy intents wicked or charitable. . . ." Having decided to risk speaking to it, however, he has to put himself in further jeopardy by following it to a secluded spot where they cannot be overheard. Horatio and the guards now become very alarmed. They think that it will tempt him onto a cliff then shift into a form so terrifying that he will go mad and hurl himself into the sea. The formerly cautious Hamlet has, however, "waxe[d] desperate" at the sight of the ghost: he is happy to risk his life, he is careless of his soul, and he is willing to kill his friends if they try to stop him. The signs are not good.

When they reach "a remote part of the platform" the apparition announces that it is his "father's spirit," doomed (in an odd mixture of popular folklore and Catholic theology) "for a certain term to walk the night/And, for the day, confin'd to waste in fires/Till the foul crimes done in my days of nature/Are burnt and purg'd away." Morning is approaching and it must soon return to the "sulphurous and tormenting flames" to which Claudius has condemned the King by cutting him off "in the blossoms of [his] sin . . . With all [his] imperfections on [his] head." The tale it tells is one of lust, murder, and betrayal, couched in the intemperate language of hate and disgust; its demands are for revenge against Claudius. But, though the apparition *says* it is the spirit of the dead king, who knows whether it is telling the truth? It seems a little confused about its exact whereabouts. Is it in purgatory, or is it in hell? It says its sins are being purged away, but its description of its present state is hellish ("I could a tale unfold whose lightest word/Would harrow up they soul; freeze thy young blood;/Make thy two eyes, like stars, start from their spheres;/Thy knotted and combined locks to part,/And each particular hair to stand on end . . .").

Hamlet himself still seems to have a lingering doubt. After it has left, his first involuntary exclamation is, "O all you host of Heaven! O earth! what else?/And shall I couple Hell?" However, he immediately brushes this thought aside and intemperately vows, on no other evidence than the word of the ghost, that his mother is a "pernicious woman" and his uncle a "smiling, damned villain." Every thought and action, he swears, will now be bent to doing the ghost's bidding; he will be consumed by the ghosts's command. The ghost exits, but later we hear his voice "beneath." Where is the ghost now? The realm beneath the earth is hell. According to Protestant theology, if the old king is in hell, he shouldn't be able to get out. The confusions may be Shakespeare's not the ghost's, but that hardly matters. The ambiguities about its whereabouts, status, and intentions would not have been lost on a contemporary audience.

The strictly correct Protestant position would be that, if the ghost is not an angelic messenger, then it must be a devil or the delusion of a sick mind. It isn't very likely that it is a delusion because Horatio and the guards have seen it too. But, if Hamlet was in his right mind before (and he seemed steady enough), he certainly seems unhinged now. From the moment he returns from speaking with the ghost, he is fraught and nervous, his words are "wild and whirling," and he seems confused, one moment alleging that "it is an honest ghost," the next trying to avoid its demands as it calls to him from the earth below and referring to it as an "old mole." He tells his friends they should not be alarmed "[h]ow strange or odd so'er I bear myself" because he will just be putting "an antic disposition on"—but what rational or strategic reason does he have for acting oddly? Could it not be that he is aware that his wits have been turned, as his friends feared, and he is trying to cover up for his peculiar behavior? Has the ghost betrayed Hamlet into madness and murder by telling devilish lies about the old king's death?

Certainly the destruction which its intervention lets loose on Hamlet, his family, and the nation does not give one confidence in its altruism. Modern directors and audiences often conclude that the tragedy unfolds because Hamlet dithers and puts off doing his duty of revenge. A contemporary audience might have come to just the opposite conclusion—that the tragedy is caused because he is rash; if he had been more circumspect, the madness and mayhem he unleashes in Denmark might have been avoided.

So, for a contemporary audience there was an interpretative option that is mostly overlooked today. For many who first witnessed it, it might seem that the tragedy was literally the work of the devil.

The Cock Lane Poltergeist

I have already recommended Andrew Lang's wonderful book *Cock Lane and Common-Sense* (1894). He drew his title from a celebrated poltergeist case that was the talk of all London in the mid-eighteenth century. It is worth looking at a famous, more or less contemporary account of this event for the light it throws on educated attitudes to ghosts and visitations in the so-called "Age of Enlightenment" in a city that was one of the most sophisticated in the world at that time.

During the eighteenth century, the development of modern science and the "mechanical philosophy" (see Easlea 1980) which accompanied it revolutionized educated men's ideas about the world and threw out the traditional concepts of several centuries. By the middle of the seventeenth century, the Royal Society was already congratulating itself for this achievement. In his history of the society, Thomas Spratt explained that:

> as for the TERRORS and MISAPPREHENSIONS which commonly . . . make men's hearts to fail and boggle at Trifles . . . from the time in which the REAL PHILOSOPHY has appear'd, there is scarce any whisper concerning such HORRORS: Every man is unshaken at those Tales, at which his ANCESTORS trembled. ([1667] 1952, 339–41)

In the face of the eighteenth century's overpowering confidence that nature was subdued and irrational fears abolished, at least in public educated men began to feel that belief in ghosts was somehow vulgar and disreputable.

In earlier centuries the world had been thought of as a semi-magical place, and strange entities such as ghosts had had their due rank and function. When the world became a machine, there was no room left for them, no possible role for them to play, no reason for them to bother people. They could only be illusory, private experiences or meaningless, inharmonious intrusions.

For the folklorist or historian of ideas, the eighteenth century creates particular difficulties, for, despite the official skepticism, at a private and personal level many people continued to believe in ghosts. Throughout the century, there was a wealth of popular occult literature. The works of seventeenth-century tractarians like Joseph Glanvil and his contemporaries Richard Bovet and George Sinclair were still to be seen in tradesmen's shops and farmers' houses and exerted a considerable influence on the minds of young people (Hutchinson 1720; see also Bovet [1684] 1951; Glanvil 1681; and Sinclair [1685] 1969). Antiquarians, too, were amassing significant amounts of information about popular concepts of the supernatural, mainly culled from village custom and country belief (notably Bourne [1725] 1977; Brand 1777; and Grose [1787] 1790). Nor was such belief confined to uneducated, rural people. There remained a significant number of educated people who still, in the privacy of their own hearts, clung to the old ideas. Keith Thomas notes, for example, that belief in ghosts was "a reality in the eighteenth century for many educated men, however much the rationalists laughed at them" (1971, 591).

It was in this sort of context—public skepticism but (at least a degree of) private belief—that the Cock Lane poltergeist excited public attention for a full five years during the mid-1700s. The knockings and scratchings at the house in Cock Lane were said to be caused by the restless spirit of the common-law wife of one Mr. K——, who was thought by many (including the lady's family) to have poisoned her in order to come by her small inheritance. The knockings emanated from a young girl, and fashionable London turned out to sit in her bedroom and listen to the manifestations. The case was discussed with all the trappings of eighteenth-century rationalism in a monograph attributed to the poet, novelist, and dramatist Oliver Goldsmith. The author's presentation of what he sees as the facts, his sneering language and dismissive logic, are just as interesting as the story itself and entirely representative of the attitudes of his age. While we must admire the passion with which he defends a defenseless man and upholds the principles of natural justice, we must note that the account contains a lot of special pleading and logical sleight of hand. All those who believe in the ghost are "credulous," "ignorant publicans," and so on; all those who disbelieve it are of the highest rank and probity.

The account is taken from the pamphlet *The Mystery Revealed* of 1742:

> [O]f all accusations . . . few seem so extraordinary, as that which has lately engrossed the attention of the public, and which is still carrying on at an house in Cock Lane near Smithfield. The continuance of the noises, the numbers who have heard them, the perseverance of the girl, and the atrociousness of the murder she pretends to detect, are circumstances that were never perhaps so favorably united for the carrying on of an imposture before. The credulous are prejudiced by the child's apparent benevolence: her age and ignorance wipe off the imputation of her being able to deceive, and one or two more, who pretend actually to have seen the apparition, are ready to strengthen her evidence. Upon these grounds, a man, otherwise of a fair character, as will shortly appear, is rendered odious to society, shunned by such as immediately take imputation for guilt, and made unhappy in his family, without having even in law a power of redress. . . .
>
> The story of the ghost is in brief, as follows: for some time a knocking and scratching has been heard in the night at Mr P———s's, where Mr K—— formerly lodged, to the great terror of the family; and several methods were tried, to discover the imposture, but without success. This knocking and scratching was generally heard in a little room, in which Mr P———s's two children lay; the eldest of which was a girl about twelve or thirteen years old. The purport of this knocking was not thoroughly conceived, till the eldest child pretended to see

the actual ghost of the deceased lady. . . . When she had seen the ghost, a weak, ignorant publican also, who lived in the neighbourhood, asserted that he had seen it too; and Mr P——s himself . . . he also saw the ghost at the same time: the girl saw it without hands, in a shrowd; the other two saw it with hands, all luminous and shining. There was one unlucky circumstance however in the apparition: though it appeared to several persons, and could knock, scratch, and flutter, yet its coming would have been to no manner of purpose, had it not been kindly assisted by the persons thus haunted. It was impossible for a ghost that could not speak, to make any discovery; the people therefore, to whom it appeared, kindly undertook to make the discovery themselves; and the ghost, by knocking, gave its assent to their methods of wording the accusation. . . . When therefore the spirit taught the assistants, or rather the assistants had taught the spirit (for that could not speak) that Mr K—— was the murderer, the road lay then open, and every night the farce was carried on, to the amusement of several, who attended with all the good-humour, which spending one night with novelty inspires; they jested with the ghost, soothed it, flattered it, while none was truly unhappy, but him whose character was thus rendered odious, and trifled with, merely to amuse idle curiosity.

To have a proper idea of this scene, as it is now carried on, the reader is to conceive a very small room with a bed in the middle, the girl at the usual hour of going to bed, is undressed and put in with proper solemnity; the spectators are next introduced, who sit looking at each other, suppressing laughter, and wait in silent expectation for the opening of the scene. As the ghost is a good deal offended at incredulity, the persons present are to conceal theirs, if they have any, as by this concealment they can only hope to gratify their curiosity. For, if they shew either before, or when the knocking is begun, a too prying, inquisitive, or ludicrous turn

"Alas, Poor Ghost!"

of thinking, the ghost continues usually silent. . . . The spectators therefore have nothing for it, but to sit quiet and credulous, otherwise they must hear no ghost, which is no small disappointment to persons, who have come for no other purpose.

The girl who knows, by some secret, when the ghost is to appear, sometimes apprizes the assistants of its intended visitation. It first begins to scratch, and then to answer questions, giving two knocks for a negative, and one for an affirmative. By this means it tells whether a watch, when held up, be white, blue, yellow, or black; how many clergymen are in the room, though in this sometimes mistaken; it evidently distinguishes white men from negroes, with several other marks of sagacity; however, it is sometimes mistaken in questions of a private nature, when it deigns to answer them: for instance; the ghost . . . called her father John instead of Thomas, a mistake indeed a little extraordinary in a ghost; but perhaps she was willing to verify the old proverb, that it is a wise child that knows its own father. However, though sometimes right, and sometimes wrong, she pretty invariably persists in one story, namely, that she was poisoned, in a cup of purl, by red arsenic, a poison unheard of before, by Mr K—— in her last illness; and that she heartily wishes him hanged.

It is no easy matter to remark upon an evidence of this nature; but it may not be unnecessary to observe, that the ghost, though fond of company, is particularly modest upon these occasions, an enemy to the light of a candle, and almost always most silent before those, from whose rank and understanding she could most reasonably expect redress. When a committee of gentlemen of eminence for their rank, learning, and good sense, were assembled to give the ghost a fair hearing, then, one might have thought, would have been the time to knock loudest, and to exert every effort; then was the time to bring the guilty to justice, and to give every possible method of information; but in what manner she behaved upon this test of her reality, will better appear from the committee's own words, than mine.

[*Here the author transcribes the overwhelmingly negative report of the investigating committee, which concludes, "It is therefore the opinion of the whole of the assembly, that the child has some art of making or counterfeiting particular noises, and that there is no agency of higher cause." The author then goes on in his own voice.*]

The ghost knows perfectly well before whom to exhibit. She could as we see venture well enough to fright the ladies, or perhaps some men, about as courageous as ladies, and as discerning; but when the committee had come up, and gathered round the bed, it was no time then to attempt at deception, the ghost was angry, and very judiciously kept her hunters at bay. . . .

The question in this case, therefore, is not, whether the ghost be true or false, but who are the contrivers, or what can be the motives for this vile deception? . . . But still it seems something extraordinary, how this imposition could be for so long carried on without a discovery. However . . . [it] was the observation of Erasmus, that whenever people flock to see a miracle, they are generally sure of seeing a miracle; they bring an heated imagination, and an eager curiosity to the scene of the action, give themselves up blindly to deception, and each is better pleased with having it to say, that he had seen something very strange, than that he was made the dupe of his own credulity.

THE CLODD/LANG DEBATE

In the annals of folklore history, probably the best-known debate between the rationalist and supernaturalist cultures is that between two of the "great team" (Dorson 1968a, 202–65) of Victorian folklorists, Andrew Lang and Edward Clodd. As their dispute is an almost perfect illustration of the debating strategies of the representatives of the traditions of belief and disbelief, it is worth describing in some detail.

Andrew Lang was not only an expert and prolific writer on ghost traditions but also a member of the Society for Psychical Research (SPR); Edward Clodd, on the other hand, was a stout-hearted rationalist who, the following year, was to scandalize Victorian society (and provoke the former prime minister of England, W. E. Gladstone, to withdraw his subscription to the Folklore Society) by arguing in his presidential address of 1896 that the rites of Christianity were but part and parcel of a long line of similar practices going back to the cult of Dionysus and beyond (Clodd 1896, 43–59). Both men were formidable debaters: the tradition of belief could have no quicker a thinker or waspish a character to represent it than Lang; the tradition of disbelief no more fearless and combative a follower than Clodd.

Battle is first joined by Clodd in his first presidential address, which included a passage that sets out to demolish the reputation of the SPR and prove that belief in spirits was mere superstition (Clodd 1895a, 78–81): "Superstitions which are the outcome of ignorance can only awaken pity," he says. Superstition disguised as science, however, merits scorn rather than pity. The SPR, by encouraging belief in the possibility of communication between the living and the dead, promulgates superstitions of this second type. What they advocate is just "barbaric spiritual philosophy." Time, space, and the laws of gravity are all ignored by its adherents, merely "untrustworthy observers" who keep their minds in water-tight compartments, "suspend or narcotize [their] judgement, and contribute to the rise and spread of another of the epidemic delusions of which history provides warning examples." "The Society will sell you not only the Proceedings . . . but glass balls of various diameters for crystalgazing from three shillings upwards." Entrenched within the dominant tradition of disbelief, Clodd does not trouble to explain the grounds for this round condemnation. He plainly feels that it is not necessary to enter into serious discussion about "the twaddle of witless ghosts"—it is simply enough to say that it is twaddle. It is not until he has to take on Lang, in fact, that he is forced to justify these opinions and discuss specific instances.

In his "Protest of a Psycho-Folklorist," Lang immediately gets his teeth into Clodd's argument, taking the latter's assertions point by point, citing cases and examples, upbraiding his president for being himself unscientific, for being led by his prejudices to miss good opportunities for useful folkloristic research, and for ignoring both tradition and empirical evidence (1895). All of these are classic strategies in the believers' repertoire.

Lang begins his attack with a deft argumentum ad hominem: "Mr Clodd asks us to contemn the 'superstitions' of Dr Alfred Wallace, Mr Crooke, Professor Lodge, Mr A. J. Balfour and all of the eminent men of science, British and foreign" who support the SPR. Lang then moves on to a blistering attack against Clodd's remarks about the sale of crystal balls:

> That many persons are so constituted as to see halluci-nations in glass balls I cannot possibly doubt, without branding some of my most intimate and least supersti-tious friends as habitual liars. I see nothing odd in a glass ball, but if I give my friends the lie, then I act as the dreamless Irish king would have done, had he called all men liars who averred that they could dream. Granting, then, that such hallucinations exist, why on earth should they not be studied like any other phe-nomenon? Is it because you can buy a ball for three shillings?

To have such hallucinations when looking into crystal balls, he argues, is just as much an individual peculiarity as, for example, having hypnagogic illusions, and "if Mr Clodd has these, he believes in their existence. Even if he has not, he probably believes because so very many people do have them." Then Lang closes in for the kill with a coup de grace typical of the tradition of belief—an appeal to superior evidence: "To everyone who thinks of it, the existence or non-existence of such subjective pictures must be a matter of evidence. I have enough to satisfy myself, and perhaps, if Mr Clodd had as much, he would be satisfied also."

The name-dropping and the appeals to human experience continue: "I have Dr Carpenter on my side." "Mr Crookes, a dis-tinguished man of science. . . ." "Australian blacks, Presbyterians, Celts, Platonists, Peruvians, Catholics, Puritan divines [were all] witnesses," "Mr E. B. Tylor . . . attended seances," "Mr Darwin's own mind was open on the matter," "countless French, German and Italian savants . . . ," "the Irish say, the Welsh say, the Burmese say, the Shanars say, the Negroes say, that there are such and such phenomena," "the evidence . . . of cameras and of the eyes of living and distinguished men . . . ," "the evidence of living and honourable men," and so on throughout the whole essay.

Lang's second line of attack focuses on the rationalist's dismissive explanations of unusual occurrences. A lighthearted suggestion of Clodd's—that psychic phenomena are the result of a disordered liver—is disingenuously taken seriously and then stood on its head: "If Mr Clodd explains all by 'a disordered liver,' then a disordered liver is the origin of a picturesque piece of folklore. That piece of knowledge is acquired for the race." This idea is then pursued in a spirit partly serious, partly humorous, Lang suggesting that a "real" scientist and a "real" folklorist would surely be hot on the trail of such vital clues to the origins of folklore:

> Take another even more extreme example, the folklore of levitation. Some man or woman is seen by witnesses, who often give evidence on oath, to rise in the air and stay therein. I have elsewhere shown that this story is as widely distributed as any *Märchen*.
>
> Then comes D. D. Home, and professes to do the trick. What an opportunity for a folklorist! One can imagine a President of the Folklore Society rushing eagerly to examine Mr Home, and to explain at once and for ever the origin of this chapter in folklore.

Clodd, he implies, would have "rushed" in the opposite direction! Similarly, on the matter of ghostly lights, another familiar motif in folklore, the SPR has collected many contemporary accounts. Rather than sneering at them, folklorists should be grateful—*especially* if Clodd is right in thinking all such accounts are mere delusions. Here is the chance to examine raw data scientifically: "with what gratitude should we thank the SPR for providing us with nascent delusions *in situ*, as it were, so that we may compare these with similar delusions in history." This is true science, he argues, and men like Tylor who attended seances "I call . . . not 'superstitious,' but 'scientific.'"

After twelve pages of detailed and spirited argument, he returns to the subject of crystal-gazing and rises to his grand finale, engaging in a last bit of name-dropping and winding up his argument about what is truly scientific:

> When psychical students are accused, *en masse*, of approaching their subjects with a dominant prejudice, the charge, to me, seems inaccurate (as a matter of fact) and, moreover, very capable of being retorted. Not the man who listens to the evidence, but the man who refuses to listen (as if he were, at least negatively, omniscient) appears to me to suffer from a dominant prejudice. . . . Of all things, modern popular science has most cause to beware of attributing prejudice to students who refuse its Shibboleth.

After this onslaught, Clodd is compelled to marshal his arguments. In his "Reply to the Foregoing 'Protest,'" he focuses his attack this time not on the content of the SPR's method— "which," he claims, "under the guise of the scientific, is pseudo-scientific" (1895b, 248), citing as an illustration the case of their "Census of Hallucinations" (Sidgwick and Johnson 1894). Still, instead of criticizing the reliability of its methods and findings (which were, indeed, suspect) he sidetracks into a typical bit of special pleading. A quarter of the accounts in the "Census," he says, were given at second hand, and, moreover, the tables show "as expected" that more women than men answered the question in the affirmative, and that "the lower the intellectual standpoint, the higher are the percentages of affirmative answers and hallucinations." Think, too, of the people who manned the inquiry, he urges:

> One tenth of the collectors were drawn from classes not highly educated, as small shopkeepers and coastguardsmen. Nor does the *personnel* of the committee itself inspire our confidence. I should prefer five thorough going skeptics to Professor Sidgwick and his wife, Miss

Alice Johnson, and Messrs Myers and Podmore (the two ladies taking, it appears, the more active share in the whole business).

After this bit of reasoning, Clodd moves on to express the conventional opinion that strange experiences need not be attributed to the operation of supernatural forces, but are most probably caused by physical or mental disorders:

> Who doubts that they are the effect of a morbid condition of that intricate, delicately-poised structure, the nervous system. . . . Voices, whether divine or of the dead, may be heard; actual figures seen; odours smelt; when the nervous system is out of gear. A mental image becomes a visual image, an imagined pain a real pain. . . . This abnormal state . . . may be organic or functional. Organic, when disease is present; functional, through excessive fatigue, lack of food or sleep, or derangement of the digestive system. . . . Only the mentally anaemic, the emotionally overwrought, the unbalanced, are the victims.

Having gone through this familiar list of naturalistic explanations for unusual occurrences and perceptions, Clodd then moves on to state in uncompromising terms the grounds on which his skepticism, and that of all adherents of the tradition of disbelief, is ultimately based: that is, the deceivability of the human senses and the willingness of unscrupulous operators to exploit that deceivability. Of levitation, for example, he argues:

> I should want the levitation repeated many times before many witnesses. I would not trust my own eyes in the matter. I cannot forget that man's senses have been his arch-deceivers, and his preconceptions their abettors, throughout human history: that advance has been possible only as he has escaped through the discipline of the intellect from the illusive impressions about phenomena which the senses convey.

Then, neatly turning the tables on Lang by quoting one of the latter's "authorities," he adds:

> And I fall back on the words of Dr Carpenter . . . "with every disposition to accept facts when I could once clearly satisfy myself that they were facts, I have had to come to the conclusion that . . . there was either intentional deception on the part of interested persons, or else self-deception. . . . There is nothing too strange to be believed by those who have once surrendered their judgement to the extent of accepting as credible things which common-sense tells us are entirely incredible.

Finally, in resounding terms, Clodd arrives at the last premise in the catalogue of traditional arguments—that, even if no rational explanation of the strange occurrences is forthcoming as yet, *in time* one will be found. Before succumbing, for instance, to tales of mystic lights, he says, we need much more "terrestrial light" on the subject, in order to find "the naturalistic explanation to which the belief must ultimately yield."

One can imagine how great Clodd's joy must have been when a great scandal hit the psychic world. Eusapia Palladino had achieved an international reputation as a medium and attracted considerable attention and support. Even the *Spectator* had given her a favorable write-up; as Clodd puts it, the journal had "indulged in 'high falutin' talk on this triumph of psychical research . . . admonishing scientific men that at their peril did they stand aloof, or still insist that the thing 'was a trick, a fraud, and nothing else.'" However, put to the test in a private sitting, Eusapia was, in Lang's colloquial phrase, "busted up"—found to be cheating (Clodd 1896, 37–40). Clodd could not help but gloat over Lang, and reserved the first part of his notorious 1896 presidential address for kicking his opponent while he was down: "that an illiterate, but astute, Neapolitan conjuror should have thus befooled men of high intellectual capacity justifies my strictures on the incompetence of scientific specialists off their own beat to detect trickery." Warming to his point, he cites other instances of deception by mediums, rejoicing, for example, that "that colossal old liar, Madame Blavatsky," was reported to have said:

> I have not met with more than two or three men who knew how to observe, and see, and remark what was going on around them. It is simply amazing! At least nine out of every ten people are entirely devoid of the capacity of observation and of the power of remembering accurately what took place even an hour before. How often it has happened that, under my direction and revision, minutes of various occurrences and phenomena have been drawn up; lo, the most innocent and conscientious people, even skeptics, even those who actually suspected me, have signed *en toutes lettres* as witnesses at the foot of the minutes! And all the time I knew that what had happened was not in the least what was stated in the minutes.

Clodd goes on to quote other instances of mediums who had been "busted up," concluding triumphantly by quoting Lang himself (from "a half-bantering letter where one hears him whistling to keep up his courage"): "It really looks as if 'psychical research' does somehow damage and pervert the logical faculty of scientific minds."

Though it looked as if luck had dealt the winning hand to Clodd, Lang did not stay down for long. Indeed, in the preface to the new edition of *Cock Lane and Common-Sense*, he had his last attempt "to make the Folk-Lore Society see that such things as modern reports of wraiths, ghosts, 'fire-walking,' 'corpse-lights,' 'crystal-gazing,' and so on, are within their province" (quoted in Dorson 1968b, 458–63). There is an element of despair, however, detectable in his complaint that:

> As he [the author] understands the situation, folklorists and anthropologists will hear gladly about wraiths, ghosts, corpse-candles, hauntings, crystal-gazing, and walking unharmed through fire, as long as these things are part of a vague rural tradition, or of savage belief. But, as soon as there is first-hand evidence of honourable men

and women for the apparent existence of any of the phenomena enumerated, then Folklore officially refuses to have anything to do with the subject. Folklore will register and compare vague savage or popular beliefs; but when educated living persons vouch for phenomena which (if truly stated) account in part for the origin of these popular or savage beliefs, then Folklore turns a deaf ear. The logic of this attitude does not commend itself to the author of *Cock Lane and Common-Sense*.

Such an attitude, he regrets, stems from the fact that minds are already closed:

> The truth is that anthropology and folklore have a ready-made theory as to the savage and illusory origin of all belief in the spiritual, from ghosts to God. The reported occurrence, therefore, of phenomena which suggest the possible existence of causes of belief *not* accepted by anthropology, is a distasteful thing and is avoided.

Somewhat wearily, he goes through the familiar arguments—testimony to the supernatural comes from "undeniably honest and absolutely contemporary" sources; not one of the explanations offered by the rationalists holds water; and the evidence for ghosts is as good as the evidence for anything else:

> We cannot expect human testimony suddenly to become impeccable and infallible in all details, just because a "ghost" is concerned. Nor is it logical to demand here a degree of congruity in testimony, which daily experience of human evidence proves to be impossible, even in ordinary matters.

Indeed, in the last resort, he argues, rationalists are as "unscientific" as they claim that believers are. Any of their explanations "is a theory like another, and, like another, can be tested" if only they would deign to do it. But they will not, for their prejudices are too deeply ingrained:

"Alas, Poor Ghost!"

Manifestly it is as fair for a psychical researcher to say to Mr Clodd, "You won't examine my haunted house because you are afraid of being obliged to believe in spirits," as it is fair for Mr Clodd to say to a psychical researcher, "You only examine a haunted house because you want to believe in spirits."

And there he rests his case.

It is not possible to say who won this dispute; there can be no victory where defeat is not conceded, just as there can be no discussion where there is no meeting of minds. Lang and Clodd simply stand either side of a great divide, entrenched in opposed traditional philosophies, using opposed traditional arguments.

We are fortunate, however, to have such a detailed record of their debate, for not only is it a fascinating chapter in the history of folklore, it also shows how even the most astute and ardent debaters do not (and perhaps cannot) step outside the arguments allotted to their team in the philosophical tug-of-war. Though cogently stated and enthusiastically expressed, their reasoning is almost entirely predictable. Lang says no more and no less than Joseph Glanvil in the seventeenth century or Margot, Violet, and Kate in the twentieth century. Clodd's opinions and arguments are just those that Lavater used four hundred years ago and those that Colette, Stella, and Enid employ today.

THE VANISHING HITCHHIKER

Oldham, 1982:

> Michael, Michael's teacher, who was a temporary, a supply teacher, they were talking one day about ghosts, and she said that her friend at Leeds had been out for the evening with a friend of hers, a gentleman friend, and they'd spent the evening in Leeds and were driving home late, very late, on a very wet, dark night, and they lived in, on the outskirts of Leeds somewhere, and as they were driving home, they passed a bus stop and there was a young girl, a youngish girl, standing at the

bus stop, and they drove straight past and then thought it was odd she should be standing there. It's so late. The buses had finished.

So, the young man said he would take her [the friend] home and then go back and see if she [the girl] was still there, and if she was still there, he would give her a lift home.

So he dropped her off and went back to the bus stop and found the young girl still there and asked if he could give her a lift home because she was getting very wet and there were no more buses that night.

So he asked her where she lived. She gave him the address, the number and the name of the street, so they set off.

Driven a little way when they got to traffic lights, and when he looked, she'd gone! Couldn't be seen! So he couldn't understand it at all.

Next morning, he went round for his friend who he'd dropped off earlier and told her what had happened.

Very perplexed about it.

So they decided to go to this address that the girl had given. Knocked at the door. An elderly lady answered and they said, "Did a young lady, her daughter or any-body, live there, because they'd given a lift to this young lady the night before, who'd given this address, and couldn't find her. She'd just disappeared and they didn't know where she was," and the old lady burst into tears and said that was her daughter who had DIED two years earlier on that same day in an accident at those traffic lights! (Story told to G. B. by Mrs. Andrea Biggs, 1983)

"The Vanishing Hitchhiker" is probably one of the best-known modern ghost stories. First brought to academic attention by a trio of articles in *California Folklore Quarterly* (Beardsley and Hankey 1942; 1943; Jones 1944b), it attracted immediate atten-tion. It has now become one of the most frequently collected and widely discussed modern stories in the world of academic folklore.

By 1993 Paul Smith and I were able list over 150 citations for the story in our bibliography of contemporary legend studies (Bennett and Smith 1993), and the number is growing daily. It has been collected from places as far apart as Algeria, Romania, and Pakistan (see, respectively, Dumerchat 1990, 266–67; Brunvand 1986, 49–50; and Goss 1984, 12), and in a variety of media—literary works, story compilations, folklore journals, *Fate* magazine, and as topical rumor reported by newspapers and heard in conversation— and it is extremely culturally variable (see, for example, Glazer 1986; 1987; Luomala 1972; Mitchell 1976; and Wilson 1975). Vanishing Hitchhikers turn up as aliens, angels, saints, Jesus, vampires, nuns, and malevolent spirits, among other things (see, respectively, Roberts 1987; Knierim 1985, 241; Cunningham 1979, 47; Fish 1976; Goss 1982, 1707; Dodson 1943; and Mitchell 1976). But in the Protestant regions of North America and Western Europe they are most often numinous beings or supernatural entities. The numinous beings usually reveal their identities by making prophecies; the supernatural entities usually turn out to be ghosts. So there are two main strands—prophesying hitchhikers and phantom hitchhikers.

In my earliest study of the "Vanishing Hitchhiker" I looked at the story in its "phantom" form, and argued that it was not really modern, as the first scholars to study it had believed, and that it was best seen in the context of a long tradition of roadside ghosts (Bennett 1984). However, I have recently come to the conclusion that, though prophesying hitchhikers indubitably are part of a very old tradition, the archetypical *phantom* hitchhiker is relatively modern after all, though by no means as "modern" as Beardsley and Hankey assumed (see Bennett 1998). I now believe there are two features of the story as told today in the Protestant West that are the result of developments in ghostlore that have taken place there in the last 100–150 years. These are the rise of the stranger-ghost and the institutionalization of the connection between ghosts and unnatural deaths.

The concept of the stranger-ghost arises to a large extent from the fracture of the supernatural world into two opposing camps, which I have discussed earlier in the context of the ghost of Hamlet's father. One of the results of this fracture was to separate purposefulness from terror. In medieval times ghosts could be both purposeful *and* terrifying. The ghosts that appeared to demand Christian burial or masses for their souls were appalling apparitions. They were so alarming that it was immediately evident that they were *ghosts*, but less obvious that they were *human*. This was still true, though to a lesser extent, with post-Reformation apparitions. Though the ghosts that appeared in the works of Glanvil, Beaumont, and Baxter at the end of the seventeenth and beginning of the eighteenth centuries were purposeful and often recognizable, they were still terrifying and there could be absolutely no doubt that they were dead. This began to change, however, in the eighteenth and early nineteenth centuries. Terrifying aspects of the supernatural began to be concentrated in purposeless hauntings, such as knockings, poltergeists, animal ghosts, and the ghosts of wicked people (who could appear in any of these guises). Purposeful apparitions began to take on a more ordinary human form and motivation. They did not need to be terrifying any more; they had long ago lost their function as a sanction for religion, and more recently had lost many of their moral functions too.

Once purposeful ghosts began to assume more lifelike human forms, it opened up the opportunity for storytellers to experiment with a new sort of supernatural encounter. If the apparition was of a person unknown to the percipient, he or she might not recognize it as a ghost and might mistake it for a living person. By the 1870s, these sorts of accounts became a standard feature of folklore collections as subsequent workers went over and over the same ground, borrowing from one another to create ever larger compilations. For these stories to work best, the percipient should be in a strange place and the ghost should not only look like a person but behave like a person. These ghosts often appeared in a particular location and assisted lost travellers. Previously, purposeful ghosts had almost invariably appeared to people who had known them in life, and had haunted people rather than locations. But the rise of the stranger-ghost changed that.

The "phantom" variants of "The Vanishing Hitchhiker" legend complex obviously depend on the stranger-ghost convention. Some of them feature purposeful ghosts who appear regularly in a certain spot to warn motorists of the bad bend in the road where they were killed. The earliest students of the legend, Beardsley and Hankey, had one in which a hitchhiking ghost saved a traveller from meeting death at the spot she herself had died (1942, 315). A similar story excited the French press in the early 1980s. It told how a girl hitchhiker warned a driver about a dangerous bend and thus saved his life before vanishing. She had, of course, been killed there (see Campion-Vincent and Renard 1992, 45; Dumerchat 1990, 257–59; Dupi 1982). There are legends, too, that are quite similar to Vanishing Hitchhiker stories in theme and structure, if not part of the same complex, notably, "The Ghost in Search of Help for a Dying Man" (Edgerton 1968). This tells how a traveller encounters somebody in the street or in a public place and is asked to undertake an errand of mercy (usually to bring a doctor or a priest to a mortally sick person). Louis C. Jones presented a couple of examples in his response to Beardsley and Hankey (1944b, 287–88), and my study of phantom hitchhikers includes a personal example which follows the familiar "Vanishing Hitchhiker" plot in almost every respect (Bennett 1984, 56).

However, phantom hitchhikers do not necessarily have to be motivated by altruism. They can be about their own affairs without regard to the living. In many stories the ghost is that of a young and beautiful woman who has been killed on the way to a dance (for a typical version see Montell 1975, 127). She does not immediately disappear but spends the evening in the traveller's company. In an example from New York State, the narrator has the traveller and ghost fix a date for the next night, then for the next; and "each night they met and played and partied at her door" (Jones 1959, 173). That these are rather incredible stories doesn't concern us; the point is that the girl has been killed while en route to a dance, but doesn't let that stop her going. Her haunting consists of a compulsive enactment of pleasures denied. In other stories the ghost is urgently trying to get home. This is sometimes explicitly written in, so; the ghost's family will explain that she will always try "to return home on her birthdays and at Christmas" (Musick 1977, 178), or the narrator will explain in his or her own voice that "it happens on rainy nights; that's when she wants to get home" (Jones 1959, 164). But what happens when the plot provides no overt motivation for the ghost to be haunting a particular place? What can a storyteller do to give the tale an acceptable beginning, middle, and end in terms of ghostly conventions?

That brings me to the second feature of the "phantom" variant of "The Vanishing Hitchhiker" that seems to me to be a relatively modern characteristic—that is, its reliance on the idea that an unnatural death may lead to a haunting. It is worth noting that it was not till the eighteenth century that sudden or unnatural death began to be seen as one of the prime reasons for the dead to be restless (a trend that was accelerated by the publication of numerous popular ghostlore compilations in the second half of the nineteenth century that largely focused on dramatic and exotic hauntings).

The connection between ghosts and suicide, murder, and untimely death is so set now in our mental habits that it seems strange to reflect that in medieval thought, and in writings of the sixteenth and seventeenth centuries, apparitions were not necessarily even of dead people. They might be wraiths of living people in dire distress, as in the famous case where John Donne "saw" his wife with a dead baby in her arms while he was abroad in France (for accounts of this case, see Aubrey 1696, chap. 5; Beaumont 1705, 107–8); or they might be emanations of the spirits of wicked people, as in Richard Baxter's famous horror story, where the stinking wraith of her depraved husband tries to get into bed with the virtuous Mrs. Bowen even though he is far away with his regiment in Ireland (Baxter [1691] 1840, 9–16, 49–52).

I think the move from medieval to modern ideas about causes of the dead being restless has to do with changing concepts of what constitutes a "bad death." In the Middle Ages, a ghost's reasons for walking were customarily linked to its postmortem experiences and underpinned the teaching of the church about the nature of the afterlife. After the Reformation, when the Protestant theology denied the existence of purgatory, ghosts tended to be restless less for what was happening to them in the afterlife and more because of what was happening to their survivors in the mundane world. So, Francis Grose describing the traditions of his grandfather's generation in his *Provincial Glossary*[1] sneeringly notes that ghosts return

"Alas, Poor Ghost!"

for some special errand such as the discovery of a murderer, or to procure restitution in land, or money unjustly withheld from an orphan or widow . . . ; sometime, the occasion of spirits revisiting this world is to inform their heirs in what secret place or private drawer in an old trunk they have hidden the title deeds of the estate, or buried their money or plate . . . . ([1787] 1790, 5–6)

So there appears to have been a gradual movement, from assessing whether a death is "good" or "bad" in terms of what happens next to the soul, to judging it in terms of what happens next to the survivors.

During the nineteenth century, this "what happens next" framework begins to be replaced with a backward-looking emphasis that primarily assesses the death in terms of the life that went before. Stories abound in legend collections about evil men who become animal ghosts or terrifying apparitions after their deaths, and have to be "laid" or tricked into bottles and thrown in the Red Sea (see, for example, Burne 1883; Hunt 1865; Ingram 1884; and Thiselton Dyer 1898). I have argued elsewhere that the evidence from contemporary ghostlore suggests that this time frame is now being squeezed in both directions towards a concept of a "bad" death which is personal and private, and the primary focus of which is the manner of dying (Bennett 1997). A corollary of this is that, whereas until perhaps the early years of the eighteenth century it was evil-doers who could not rest in their graves, nowadays it is the victims who are restless.

Be that as it may, by the end of the nineteenth century, in Britain at least, the relationship between apparitions and untimely or violent deaths was just assumed, and ghosts were thought to haunt the living either because they had been cut off so quickly that they had left necessary business unfinished, or because they had had a death so cruel or violent that the death itself could not die and went on being reenacted. Similar patterns are observable in stories collected in America in the early twentieth century. Louis C. Jones's study of the ghosts of New York, for example, shows that more than a third died violent or sudden deaths (1944a), and in Rosalie Hankey's article on California ghosts, murder and suicide top the list of reasons given for non-malevolent ghosts to walk (1942).

"The Vanishing Hitchhiker" in its "phantom" form fits this pattern so well that it can be used as a case study of what a "bad death" might mean today for many people in America and Western Europe. The first element of the "bad death" as depicted in these stories is sudden and violent death. Most of the phantom hitchhikers have died in road traffic accidents, though less frequently she (or he; there are many examples of male hitchhikers, see Bennett 1998) has been murdered or is the victim of a horrific death. One girl dies in a house fire; a man is stuffed in a barrel and rolled downhill; an old lady is cemented into a barn floor; and so on.

The second element is the concept of an "undeserved" death. Most of the ghosts are stereotypically innocent characters—loving husbands, caring mothers, and beautiful daughters—yet all die by accident or violence. In an American story, there are a whole family of hitchhikers, pious pioneers murdered on the way home from a prayer meeting (Musick 1977, 76). In another, the hitchhiker is a young husband on the way to see his first child (Fonda 1977). In a story taken up by the U.K. press in 1977, the hitchhiker is a young man, who may have been an innocent victim of the notorious "hanging judge," Judge Jeffries, or "the spirit of an American serviceman killed in a car crash" (Goss 1984, 64–67).

The third element in concepts of the "bad death" is to be cut off in one's prime, cheated of the future and the joys it might offer. The archetypical phantom hitchhiker is that archetypical victim, a young, vulnerable, and beautiful girl on the verge of adulthood. This concept comes out most strongly in the versions where the girl has been killed on the way to or from a dance. Though these are not very numerous, I would suggest that this theme implicitly underlies many other Vanishing Hitchhiker stories in its "phantom" form, especially the American ones. Nearly all the stories where the ghost is a girl stress her clothing, which is almost invariably appropriate to a dance—a "lavender evening dress," a "long gown," a "black velvet cape," and so on. (In Britain this theme is more often represented by stories of girls who are killed on the way to their wedding; see, for example, the "Blue Bell Hill" ghost described in Goss 1984, esp. 106–8.)

The fourth element in the picture of modern Western notions about what it means to die badly is the notion of dying alone. Unless they are returning to their graves or on the way to a dance, these ghosts are out on the highway in the hope of getting home. Indeed, the plot often pivots on the ghost giving a specific address where it wants to be taken. Waiting at home, there is always a grieving relative. If postmortem behavior as depicted in ghost stories reliably indicates what sorts of death are to be avoided—and I think it does—then narratives about ghosts who are restless because they died away from home, and which perpetually attempt to reenter the family circle, indicate the importance attached today to not dying alone. Of course, none of these address-giving ghosts ever does get home; every journey is futile. They disappear from the car every time before they can get to their destination. Nevertheless, they never give up trying.

Lastly, I want to suggest that there is a sense in which these stories show that many people in the U.K. and America today implicitly believe that *any* death is "bad." These ghosts are totally secular and cannot be fitted into a religious scheme. There is no lesson to be learned by their lives, no moral to be pointed out by their deaths. Nor is there any "place" from which they have returned. Indeed, it would be silly to ask where they have come from. Ghostly hitchhikers are plainly neither in hell nor in heaven. Their heaven was on earth; their hell is that they have been forced precipitately to leave it. Their exemplary characters, and social position as the new father, the bride-to-be, the promising student, or the beautiful girl, are just ways of emphasizing the cruelty of death.

In a sense, then, the underlying assumption of all these stories is that it is death itself that is "bad." And that may be a distinctly modern point of view.

A Brief History of "Witnesses"

I want to end by returning to the concept of the souls of the dead as "witnesses" of the lives of the living. Witnesses accomplish changes in the mundane world through some form of indirect intervention by means of some sort of communication with the living. In one way this makes them a very traditional form of revenant; their purposefulness links them, for example, to the interfering and loquacious ghosts of the seventeenth century. But the low-key encounters, the domesticity of the witnesses' interests, the humdrum little affairs with which they concern themselves—all these seem to cut them off from the ghosts of the "public" tradition.

Conventional ghost stories have a dramatic quality that can be continuously used and reused—as ammunition in philosophical or religious arguments, as motifs in works of art, as entertainment, thrills, and horrors, and as a means of making money. "The Vanishing Hitchhiker" legend has been used, or may be used, in any of these ways. Such stories therefore turn up time and time again in both educated and popular literature, and in films and TV series. In these media, they are shaped with great skill to make unforgettably impressive accounts that can serve a variety of useful purposes. Though they continue to be folklore, they are also a part of popular and educated culture, and are thus highly visible. "Witnesses" who hide pension books or help paint houses are not a part of this "public" canon. They are much less visible, and they seem far removed both from the purposeful ghosts of the past with their religious or social missions and their potential for menace and from the usual run of ghost stories circulating in the oral tradition. However, before judging that this lively belief is exclusively modern (or, indeed, just an oddity of the folklore of elderly women living in the UK), there are several points which have to be considered. By reading and detective work, the ancestry of quiet and personal purposeful ghosts may be established just as clearly as that of the more visible beliefs (though we should remember that the themes, motifs, and functions of these stories may differ from that of tales about vanishing hitchhikers or the Cock Lane poltergeists).

Some early impressionistic evidence that the witness type may have a lineage in older folklore is provided by a comparison of the lexis of representative texts. A word list compiled from witness stories in this book shows that the twenty-five terms most frequently used by narrators are (in order of frequency) "dead," "feel," "see," "mother," "father," "think," "say," "come," "alive," "there," "house," "plainly," "happen," "bedroom," "bed," "husband," "know," "(a)wake(n)," "night," "as though," "tell," "presence," "always," "help," and "lost." This list is surprisingly close to one compiled from John Aubrey's *Miscellanies* of 1696.

Of all the writers whose works have been discussed here, Aubrey—rambling, discursive, and credulous—is the closest to the folklore of his time; and of his writings, it is the stories in the *Miscellanies* that give the best indication of having been taken verbatim, or almost verbatim, from the mouths of living (and believing) informants. It is significant, therefore, that in this book, the words most frequently used in connection with "apparitions," "spirits," and "ghosts" (as he calls them) are "dead," "bed," "say," "saw," "ask," "tell," "(a)wake(n)," "vanish," "friend," "wife," "look," "appear," "go," "come," "fancy," "advise," "alive," "dream," "nothing," "ill," and "noise." One-third of the words in the two lists therefore are identical, another six are related ("mother," "father," and "husband" reflect female orientations to kinship, "friend" and "wife," male orientations; the modern phrase "as though he was there" is roughly comparable to the older "fancy that he appeared"; and "help" is not dissimilar to "advise"). Where differences do occur, they are primarily in the degree of the subjectivity or objectivity of the report, rather than the content. Shorn of the elaborations typical of the period, the essence of Aubrey's old stories is surprisingly similar to that of the modern memorates, the emphasis in both cases being on the presence of the dead person in familiar form, on its being there (and sometimes visible), on the communication with it, and on the cause or result of the encounter. This indicates that many of the assumptions about such visitations have remained surprisingly constant in spite of changes in surface detail, in literary and oral styles, and in cultural climate.

Indeed, four of Aubrey's stories directly feature apparitions that have strong affinities with the witnesses of modern tradition. One concerns the will of Sir Walter Long of Draycot. On three occasions when a clerk tries to draft a paper which will disinherit her son in favor of the children of Sir Walter's second marriage, the phantom hand of the first Lady Long is seen hovering reproachfully over the paper. In a second story, the spirit of a dead first wife appears to show the place where the settlement on her children is hidden and thus they gain their inheritance. Here we plainly have the motif of the dead mother still active to protect those she loved in life. We are really not a far cry from Rachel's house-painting brother (also concerned about justice for survivors) or Elisabeth's dead husband (also willing to remind her of the whereabouts of lost documents).

Elsewhere in Aubrey's collection, we find ghosts who effect cures. Though the surface detail of these stories—weird strangers, ghosts, recipes, ague—is unfamiliar, the underlying idea that the dead have power to help and cure the living is as evident there as it is in witness traditions. In one of Aubrey's stories—the truth of which is vouched for by the Archbishop of Canterbury!—an old man is kind to a mysterious stranger dressed in outlandish clothes "not seen or known in those parts" and, in gratitude, the stranger cures his lameness. In another, a ghost appears with an eccentric remedy for ague (to lie on one's back from ten to one daily). The window dressing is different but the theme is very similar to Ruth's and Ella's, perhaps related, accounts in which a "lady in white" comes to a sick child and tells her to get better.

A book written some thirty or forty years after Aubrey's *Miscellanies* provides further evidence of the existence of some sort of "witness" tradition in times gone by. In 1729, that great journalist, publicist, and exploiter of popular tastes, Daniel Defoe, under the alias "Andrew Moreton," was compiling his most famous work on the supernatural, *The Secrets of the Invisible World Disclos'd*. At the outset, he puts forward the proposition that "almost all real apparitions are of friendly and assisting angels and come of a kind and beneficent Errand" (Defoe 1729, 26). He carefully explains that the mistake in learned thinking is "that we either will allow no apparition at all, or will have every apparition to be of the Devil; as if none of the Inhabitants of the World above, were able to show themselves, or had any Business among us" (ibid, 16). Defoe's bracketing together of "assisting angels" and the souls of the dead, his talk of "kind and beneficent Errands" and "Inhabitants of the World above" directly reflect the Manchester women's phraseology about witnesses, and his argument that the dead do indeed "show themselves" here and have "Business among us" is precisely the rationale of their beliefs.

It is difficult to follow the trail of the witness through the rest of the eighteenth century and the early decades of the nineteenth century. By the 1730s, educated opinion was firmly set against the concept of supernatural powers and there is a gap in serious writing on the subject from then till at least the turn of the century. One of the best guides to the supernatural folk beliefs of the early nineteenth century is Catherine Crowe's two-volume compilation of precognitive and ghost experiences, *The Night-Side of Nature* 1848). Mrs. Crowe brings together a massive collection of narratives and a body of theoretical speculation placing traditional texts higgledy-piggledy alongside memorates, family stories, and contemporary rumors. Unusually for the period, her work gives a very clear idea of what were the continuing traditions of the time and what was currently considered to be believable. In her narratives, ghosts can be seen paying debts, revealing murders, and returning because they died with something on their mind, but one of the commonest themes is the return of parents to offer love and comfort.

These ideas continued to appear in some of the better literature in the early decades of the twentieth century (I specially like Giraud 1927; Lewes 1911; and Wood 1936). These texts offer continuing evidence to suggest that ghosts who return out of love for family or home, or in order to serve the interests of their survivors, were a steady feature of the supernatural image at that time.

It is significant that, in his 1959 study of American ghostlore, Louis C. Jones lists one of the five principal types of ghost behavior as warning, consoling, informing, guarding, or rewarding the living. Similarly, a study undertaken in Britain in 1956 by the Society for Psychical Research found that three-quarters of the apparitions they documented had been seen by some person who had a strong personal bond with the dead person ("Six Theories about Apparitions" 1956).

More up-to-date evidence from America can be found in two papers by folklorist Larry Danielson (1979; 1983). Danielson notes that the majority of the apparitions in his study of paranormal memorates culled from archive transcriptions, folklore collections, popular paperbacks, and *Fate* magazine "appear to some person with whom the appearer has some strong emotional bond" (1983, 201). They "are purposeful, most often involved in helpful missions to the living" (ibid, 201), and generally appear when the percipient is "in a critical condition, psychological or physical" (ibid,

198). Danielson notes that his findings closely correspond with those in analyzed surveys from 1890 to 1962.

A final, contingent piece of evidence for traditions of friendly, visiting ghosts comes from Ireland. Among many accounts of frightening apparitions and alarming hauntings in the archive of the Ulster Folk and Transport Museum, Linda-May Ballard reports the following more pleasant belief. The informant explains that:

> on . . . Holly Eve [Halloween] you would . . . they used to sweep up the ashes and clean the floor all round, and in near the grate here they would leave a lock of ashes, and smooth it down, and when they came down in the morning they would see the tracks of the feet, where they would be sitting, warming themselves. . . .

Quoting this account, Ballard observes that it blends folk and religious tradition together and appears to be "an act of affection . . . the dead being welcomed into the house" (1981, 29–30).

Each of these bits of information contributes a piece to the jigsaw picture of the friendly witnessing ghost. The Irish account shows dead people returning to their homes and welcomed there; the American surveys indicate the helpfulness of the visitation and the bonds between visitor and visited; Crowe's stories have all these features; Defoe's and Aubrey's earlier writings specify the kinds of errand the dead may carry out in their role as "assisting angels" in the world of the living.

Throughout all the accounts run threads that link the humble witness of modern tradition to the great ghosts of the past—their active purposefulness, their awareness of events transpiring in the earthly domain, and their power for good in the lives of former loved ones. The idea of the "witness" is thus the epitome of a philosophy that sees the creation as whole, ordered, hierarchical, harmonious, and more than a little magical.

Appendix 1

Collecting the Data

Working out what sort of data you need, and how you can set about getting it, are both crucial to the success of any enterprise. But they are by no means easy decisions. This chapter presents the methods used to obtain the data on which this book is based.

The bulk of the material was collected in Manchester, Northwest England, in the early 1980s; most of that in chapter 3 was collected in the English East Midlands in the late 1990s. The accounts below do not set out to be templates and should not be used as guides to good practice; they are simply personal records.

The Manchester Study

As I noted in the introduction, this book grew out of a doctoral dissertation which set out to evaluate the role of storytelling, legend, and memorate in the formation and expression of belief. Uncomfortable with the commonplace assumption that legends accurately represent folk belief, I wanted to put people in a position where they had to affirm or deny belief in an important, but controversial, matter. Nothing could be a more important but more disputed idea than that the dead can interact with the living; so it was this topic that I chose for my research.

Originally I tried to make a general appeal for informants who could be interviewed in their own homes. I made my approach via the press, preparing a short informative piece and sending it off to local and national newspapers. It was not a success. In the first place, my own introductory item was never used; instead, the papers wrote their own copy, often accompanied by lurid and ridiculous headlines ("Scare me silly, says Gilly," was the Sheffield *Star*'s effort). In the second place, very few people wrote in, and most of those plainly only wanted a visitor or did not sound like the sort of people one should visit alone. I fared no better with a couple of interviews I did for local radio. So I abandoned this plan very quickly. Then I briefly toyed with the idea of trying a survey round the university campus, but soon realized it would not be any more successful.

After some thought, I concluded that this sort of approach would never work. What I needed was a situation where I could talk to people in a reasonably natural situation. I had done the research for my master's degree in a city center pub; but, though the atmosphere was relaxed and conducive to storytelling and personal talk, the resulting tapes had been a nightmare to transcribe because of the level of noise from surrounding conversations, loud music, and people banging glasses down in front of the microphone. I was reluctant to use that sort of venue again. As alternatives, I thought of trying a hairdresser's salon, a beauty parlor, or a health club, but there were technical problems with all of these venues too.

Eventually I hit on the idea of asking my father, who, after fourteen years at the same podiatrist's practice, was nearing retirement, to let me talk with his patients during surgery hours. This worked extremely well, resulting in 132 taped interviews, and a total of 208 narratives (143 memorates, 25 personal experience stories on general topics, 33 contemporary legends, and 7 accounts of local happenings both natural and supernatural).

My father's surgery was situated near the center of a middle-class suburb, near the busy "village," as the area where the shops and services are located is called; it was therefore convenient for local residents, and this, together with my father's loveable nature, ensured a large and thriving practice drawing from all sections of the community. In a podiatrist's clinic, conversation is considered courteous and necessary, and often is of a fairly intimate nature. My father was used to receiving confidences, discussing politics, religion, and philosophy, giving practical advice, and hearing domestic and marital troubles. He himself had a great interest in parapsychology and I knew he had often discussed the reality of psychic powers and supernatural experiences with his patients. Only recently he had told me about strange occurrences which patients had discussed with him while the events were still fresh in their minds.

So, in many respects my father's status was that of an informal counsellor, and his surgery a sort of confessional or advice bureau. Several factors led to this situation. A visit to a podiatrist will take approximately twenty minutes and will have to be regularly maintained, in many cases over years rather than months. Secondly, foot care is by its nature personal and somewhat intimate—and surprisingly relaxing. Finally, many of his patients were part of the same social network based on the neighborhood; many used the same doctor as my parents, went to the same church, and shopped at the same local shops. With the patients' permission, I simply sat in on their treatment, told them what I was researching and how I was planning to use the material, and recorded everything that was said. Each session lasted the full twenty minutes; otherwise the framework was very flexible and open-ended. Though I had drawn up a checklist of questions for my own use, I did not refer to it, or have it with me. As the purpose was to invite natural conversation, I used it only to initiate talk; if respondents seemed wary or alarmed by any topic, I skipped it and homed in on those they were eager to talk about. I was not aiming for a statistical analysis. As luck would have it, though, I did have sufficient answers on the majority of questions to permit an overview.

I agreed with my father that he should not enter the conversation, or try to direct his patients' responses, or interrupt if they were in full flow. However, he soon got into the habit of joining in with query, observation, or story of his own if conversation flagged, as any good interviewer would, and soon we developed an easy, pleasant, and productive partnership. No one refused to talk to me (though I gave them every chance to do so) and only a very few were wary and distrustful; most regarded me as a welcome, though unusual, sort of in-house entertainment. Many told me how much they had enjoyed the visit.

By working with my father I was able to exploit an already existing situation and structure the interviews as relaxed, informal conversations in which there was seldom any sense of artificiality or strain. In fact, my presence pointed up the occasion in two significant ways—by increasing the sense of social occasion and by focusing discussion and storytelling. Though my father had already heard many of the narratives his patients told me, there were very many that were completely new to him; and though he was aware of his patients' personal philosophies, he commented that he had seldom heard them so expansively and cogently explained. The presence of a third person seems in this way to have enhanced rather than destroyed the social context out of which story and discussion usually flowed. I therefore believe that these conversational interviews provide a solid body of information about the forms discourse takes when its context is the discussion of belief, opinion, and philosophy.

What seemed to be particularly helpful was not only that the interview was kept friendly and relaxed (informants themselves often turning questioner and asking for *my* opinions), but also that, as the study progressed, I could adapt the wording of my questions and prompts to fit in with the phraseology people themselves used (see chapter 1). Following their linguistic clues, I dropped questions about the "supernatural" and "belief in ghosts" in favor of "the mysterious side of life" and "THINGS in houses." This had a marked effect on the responses I received, supplanting denial or even fear with openness and eagerness to share.

A final, very important, advantage of informal conversational interviews such as I was able to conduct is that informants do not have to be pressed to give clear yes or no answers as they would for a written questionnaire or formal survey. Very often they like to phrase their answers with a little face-saving ambiguity (see Hufford 1977). In these circumstances, if they are pushed to say whether "I think there may be something in it" means "definitely yes" or "definitely no," they will probably say "no," even though that is not their real opinion. Also, the approach allows informants to express partial belief as well as unashamed conviction, and that gives a fairer and more accurate picture overall. There are problems here, of course. If the informant will not herself plainly answer "yes" or "no," the researcher is left to make the judgments (with the danger of getting it all wrong). With practice, however, one can learn to pick up linguistic clues which are quite reliable guides to belief or disbelief. These clues are set out in diagrammatic form in appendix 4.

Altogether I worked in my father's surgery for five afternoons a week for five months until he retired. Early on in my fieldwork it became apparent that elderly women were going to outnumber other people, and that I had no hope of achieving balanced numbers for age and sex. This is because elderly women not only constitute the bulk of a podiatrists' patients, but are at home during the day and therefore are more likely than other people to make appointments during the afternoon (which was when I myself was able to get to the surgery); and also, perhaps, because elderly women choose an elderly medical man? On reflection, however, I decided that this skewing towards one sex and age group did not matter; it offered me the chance to study a small but fairly homogeneous sample, pretty well matched for age, sex, social class, and, to a lesser extent, religion. After a month or two, I therefore stopped interviewing either men or women under sixty years old. By the end of my research period, I had interviewed 96 retired women, 20 women between 40 and 60 years old, 3 young girls, and 13 elderly men. I set aside the interviews with the three latter groups and also 9 early interviews where I had made mistakes of vocabulary and approach. The beliefs of the remaining 87 elderly women formed the focus of the Manchester study.

With hindsight it is easy to see that the research project was both difficult and ambitious. It was difficult in that the subject matter was delicate and at every step it was possible to offend or alarm the respondents or misrepresent their opinions. Only after it had begun did it become apparent just how sensitive an area supernatural beliefs can be, and how many pitfalls lie in wait for the unwary. It is obviously not the sort of project to enter into lightly; I can now see only too clearly why many researchers have preferred a more distant, less personal approach to the documentation of beliefs. Thanks to the cooperation of my family, however, I feel that I managed to create one of the very few research situations in which frank replies can be obtained to sensitive questions.

THE LEICESTER STUDY
(contributed by Dr. Kate Bennett, De Montfort University, Leicester, U.K)

I was responsible for designing the research, finding and contacting a suitable research-group, devising a questionnaire, and coordinating the fieldwork and transcriptions. As is usual in my field, the interviews and transcriptions were undertaken by paid workers.

Sally Pearson, who did the interviewing, is a psychology graduate studying for a masters in forensic psychology. She had some experience of interviews and a good insight into mental health issues. Stephanie Vidal-Hall, who did the transcription, was then a part-time lecturer at De Montfort in the Department of Performing Arts. She is a close and trusted friend who, while not having any formal psychology training, is "a child of the manse" and therefore well-accustomed to confessionals. She has good interpersonal skills and a marked "feel" for the data.

The respondents were all members of a club for widowed women which meets on Sunday afternoons in Leicester, a city in the English East Midlands. The genesis of this group is interesting in itself and also useful in giving some sort of idea of the type of people who were consulted for this study. Grieving people are often urged to join support groups such as the Widow to Widow program in the U.S. or, in the U.K., Cruse[1] for widows or Compassionate Friends for those who have lost children (for discussions of self-help groups, see Lieberman 1993; Prosterman 1996), but this sort of formal or semiformal organization geared to counselling does not suit everyone:

- ... everyone doesn't want Cruse. There's one going in Leicester now. Well, I went to the first meeting, and there was a vicar— Well, I don't know what HE knew about widowhood!— and somebody else that was married, so SHE wouldn't know much about it! And they seemed so— On the committee— they had a committee, and they all seemed to know what was right for you. Well, you don't want counselling, you want friendship, you want somewhere to go, and just somebody to talk to you. You don't want these people— I suppose they're well up in their profession but that's what— you don't want. People don't want religion either. (Mrs. G, transcript, 23–24)

Many widows also don't want to get involved with the singles scene even if they are craving company or a partner for the dancing that seems to be a large part of the social lives of many of them:

- But you see, we found though there was plenty of things if you were over sixty, there was nothing under sixty unless you go to these clubs and these singles places, and I went there once and I felt dirty. Honestly, they were just women looking to pick up men and men picking up women. It was! I come home and I thought, "Well, that's not for me." (Mrs. G, transcript, 13–14)

The answer for many bereaved women is an informal club where they can go to meet people in a similar situation just to talk and be in the company of others. The Leicester group goes on outings and takes holidays together, and meets for tea and talk on Sundays (hence their informal name for themselves, "The Sunday Widows"). As a founder-member said:

- I found that there wasn't anything for anybody under sixty, anywhere to go, not on your own, and then [another founder-member] put it in the paper, an advert that said "Found that Sunday was a blighted day of the week for widows? Would anybody be interested?" I'd got a daughter that'd just finished— and she said to me, "Are you going?" "No way," I says. "No way." But anyway, she says, "Oh, come on!" and I went, and I think there was probably about fifty, about fifty people there. That was the start, and the church then— we were up at the church, the Baptist church. The vicar there was very, very helpful to us. It was nothing religious about it, because a lot of us didn't want that, and we started there and then. We formed a committee, and we had a cup of tea and a biscuit, kind of thing, and then we just started off there. (Group interview, transcript, 3–4)

When the Leicester study was first envisaged, it was the charity Age Concern that was first contacted. Though unable to help directly, they mentioned the widows' group, and supplied the telephone number of the chairwoman (Mrs. A). She was immediately interested, negotiated with the other members, facilitated the project, and made arrangements for the group meeting that concluded this phase of the study.

The data consists of tape-recorded interviews with nineteen[2] widows between ages sixty and seventy-six who had been widowed between two and twenty-six years. They were interviewed in their own homes over a six-month period during 1997–98. The interviews lasted from one to four hours, the average being about an hour and a half.

Age Concern told me about the widows club and gave me Mrs. A's telephone number. When I finally got in touch with her (she was always out!) she was very interested and almost immediately offered to help. I then wrote her a letter explaining what the study was about and she discussed this with the ladies at the next meeting of the Leicester Widow's Sunday Club. They agreed to invite me to come and give a talk at the club, and also for me to invite them to participate. Next I sent Mrs. A a package of material to be distributed. This included a letter of introduction, an information sheet, an "expression of interest" form and a stamp-addressed envelope. I think Mrs. A distributed between forty and sixty and I had twenty-one replies (one of which I couldn't trace later), so twenty interviews took place. Nineteen of these were coherent enough for transcription and coding.

I did the interview with Mrs. A before training Sally to interview. I also sought help from a colleague (Dr. Noon) on the design of the interview. Ethics approval was given by Leicestershire Health Authority (the ethical body acting for De Montfort). When the replies were received, Sally telephoned the respondent to arrange an interview. She explained what it entailed and again asked for the opportunity to interview. The group interview took place one afternoon at De Montfort when most of the interviews had been completed. I did the interviewing on this occasion.

Sally was asked to use the schedule as a loose guide, but was told to follow up interesting leads if she felt that was important and to avoid closed questions. On the whole avoiding closed questions was straightforward. However, when discussing emotional responses, this was often more difficult. Nevertheless, where closed questions were used, they generally did not elicit a one word answer; rather, the responses were as if the question had been an open one. Although the schedule asked some factual questions, in practice Sally did not record them on paper, just on tape, so some interviews miss this information and the tape appears to start mid sentence. This is an area I would want to be more careful about next time. Sally was expected to ask about the key themes of the interview, but to use the prompts only if she needed to. I was not interested in being prescriptive; my interest was in learning from the widows what was important to them. My approach was "I am the novice and they are the experienced."

The Leicester women were sixty years of age or over, and had been widowed between two and twenty-six years. Two women had been married and widowed twice. I did not ask questions about social class and occupation. However, my general impression is that most of these women were working class and had worked outside the home (though not as the main bread winner) when they were younger. They had also been the principal homemaker and had looked after the children of the marriage.

The interviews were tape-recorded and undertaken in the respondents' own homes; they were semi-structured and lasted between three-quarters of an hour and an hour-and-a-half. One respondent was interviewed twice, on both occasions between an hour and an hour-and-a-half. Before beginning the interview, the respondent was given an information sheet to read and asked to sign a consent form; confidentiality and anonymity were assured. The interviewer began with an introductory formula to the effect of: "Thank you for agreeing to talk about your experiences of widowhood. I am interested in your personal experience, and it may be different from other people's, so tell me what it has been like for you. The interview will last between one and one-and-a-half hours. I would like to tape record the conversation with your permission. We will be able to arrange an opportunity for you to hear the tape if you would like. Should you wish to stop the interview at any time, or take a break, please tell me."

The interview schedule consisted of five parts: first factual questions concerning age, length of marriage, widowhood and family relations; then four sections enquiring about the widow's life at various times.

The first of the middle sections asked about what the marriage had been like. Questions included what hobbies they had done together, what the division of labour had been, what had they done separately, did they argue and so on. The second section asked about the time around the death of their husbands. For example, they were asked to describe what a typical day had been like after the death, whether they went out, what support they had had from family and friends, how they had felt, and what emotions they had experienced. The next section asked them what they did and how they felt one year on. They were asked how their lives had changed by then, what a typical day was like at that stage, whether they were now doing anything new, whether anything had changed with regards to work around the home. They were asked had their feelings changed, whether they were lonely or whether they enjoyed being able to spend time alone. The last section asked about what their lives were like at the present time. What did they do with their time, how did they feel about their widowhood, how had their lives changed, what their emotions were, and how they felt now about being alone.

The question about the "presence of the dead" was asked whenever the context seemed to allow it to be broached (on two occasions a suitable opening never presented itself). It was always couched in vague and neutral terms, such as "Do you ever feel he's still around?" "Do you ever feel his presence?" and so on. Sometimes this context was particularly poignant.

Appendix 2

Transcribing Spoken Texts

Collections of stories made from field recordings, as the memorates in this book were, can be quite difficult to handle. Spoken English is full of false starts, digressions, hesitations, repetitions, and non sequiturs. People do not necessarily signal the grammatical relationships of clauses or other chunks of discourse. Instead, they tend to string ideas loosely together and leave the hearer to sort out the logic that binds them together. Again, speakers assume they and their listeners share a common background, so logical links are often omitted; yet, on the other hand, they seem never to assume they will be believed, so their speech is packed with details of the "It was Wednesday. No, I tell a lie. It must have been Monday because I was doing the washing, and our Brenda had just popped in to say she was expecting twins" variety. None of this matters in conversation (unless it is carried to excess), but, as soon as real speech is copied down word for word and set on the printed page, it looks uncouth and comical, and it is sometimes hard to follow what is going on. We simply are not aware that we really do speak like that, for we are a literate society and are used to the neatness and finish of written English. A story, transcribed exactly as it was told, may seem strange or make wearisome reading.

In the past, therefore, it was the practice to rewrite oral narratives, preserving the story, but tidying up the wording, tightening the narrative line, and generally "improving" it so that it acquired literary shape and polish. The Brothers Grimm, for example, in successive editions of their *Nursery and Household*

Tales bowdlerized texts, amalgamated versions, joined up story fragments to make new wholes, introduced direct speech and proverbial expressions, and generally reinvented the stories in ways that they judged would render them "purer," more "authentic" and more "German," as well as more interesting (Briggs 1993, 392–407; see also Ellis 1987). And they were not alone: this, or something like it, was the practice throughout the nineteenth century and well into the present one in the English-speaking world too. The result of all this "improving" is a neat, readable narrative like the following account of "The Guardian Black Dog" in Augustus Hare's *The Story of My Life*:

Brancepeth Castle, 3 January, 1885

> Mr Wharton dined. He said, "When I was at the little inn at Ayscliffe, I met a Mr Bond, who told me a story about my friend Johnnie Greenwood, of Swancliffe. Johnnie had to ride one night through a wood a mile long to the place he was going to. At the entrance of the wood a large black dog joined him, and pattered along by his side. He could not make out where it came from, but it never left him, and when the wood grew so dark that he could not see it, he still heard it pattering beside him. When he emerged from the wood, the dog had disappeared, and he could not tell where it had gone to.
>
> Well, Johnnie paid his visit, and set out to return the same way. At the entrance of the wood, the dog joined him, and pattered along beside him as before; but it never touched him, and he never spoke to it, and again, as he emerged from the wood, it ceased to be there.
>
> "Years after, two condemned prisoners in York Gaol told the chaplain that they had intended to rob and murder Johnnie that night in the wood, but that he had a large dog with him, and when they saw that, they felt that Johnnie and the dog together would be too much for them.
>
> "Now that is what I call a useful ghostly apparition," said Mr Wharton. (Hare [1896] 1986, 5:425)

This is very nice, very entertaining, very well told, but many students of oral narrative would feel that it has been "homogenized"—that everything individual, idiosyncratic, and intrinsically *oral* has been taken out, so that it is indistinguishable from a literary narrative. Indeed, it has *become* literature.

From the 1960s, therefore, scholars of oral narrative increasingly moved toward presenting texts which looked more genuinely "oral." First came texts which were left *almost* as originally spoken: only the "um's" and "er's," the false starts, and the hesitations were taken out so that the story could be followed and due credit given to the skill of the storyteller. This seems, for example, to have been Richard Dorson's practice in his collection of American folklore, *Buying the Wind* (1964).

The representation of speech as spoken was then carried a step further, scholars seeking to put something *extra* into their transcriptions as well as take *less* out of them. The consensus was that bare texts were nothing, mere shadows of their meaningful selves, if only the words were represented (however faithfully). What was needed was as full an indication as possible of paralinguistic and supralinguistic features. The "ethnopoetic" approach to Native American texts in work like Dell Hymes's *"In Vain I Tried to Tell You"* (1981) and Dennis Tedlock's *The Spoken Word and the Work of Interpretation* (1983) was particularly influential. The aim was to produce "a performable script" (Tedlock 1983, 62). Tedlock urged that the stories he published should be read aloud from his transcriptions (1972). More recently, scholars such as Elizabeth Fine and Bill Ellis in the U.S., as well as Herbert Halpert and J. D. A. Widdowson in their work on Newfoundland folk narrative, have also argued that texts should be transcribed not only absolutely verbatim, but also with as many paralinguistic and kinesic features as possible indicated (Ellis 1987; Fine [1984] 1994; Halpert and Widdowson 1984; 1996).

During the course of a professional life when one of my main interests has been the analysis of storytelling techniques, I have experimented with several different ways of representing speech and the interchange of discourse. For my early work on contemporary legend, I used the convention of normalizing the text just a little but leaving the "um's and er's" in (see, for example, Bennett 1984);

I then began to add capitals or italics into the transcriptions to show stress and/or changes of tempo; and for my later work I adapted the transcription system developed by sociological discourse analyst Gail Jefferson because it is good at showing paralinguistic features, social interaction, and overlapping voices (Sacks, Schegloff, and Jefferson 1978; and see Bennett 1989a; 1989b; and especially 1993). There are advantages in all these practices. As always, much depends on the purpose for which the transcription is being made; and, of course, it must be recognized that none of theses transcriptions is "transparent"; each one represents a different sort of re-creation—the author's own creation—of the original story.

In spite of the reprinting of Fine's book (and Halpert and Widdowson's more recent acclaimed rich-text edition of Newfoundland folktales), many scholars are now turning away from the practice of trying to interpret a speaker's intention and represent it on the printed page. The impetus comes principally from postmodernist reservations about the political nature of all scholarly representations (though it also might have something to do with the difficulty of producing "verbatim" texts and the unreadability of the result). Clifford Geertz, for example, has consistently pointed out that ethnographic writings can never be windows on society, transparently revealing lives exactly as lived or tales exactly as told; the anthropologist him- or herself gets in the way. The one who studies is as omnipresent as the one studied, or more so. Ethnographic writings are necessarily constructs of the writer, authorial creations—just a different sort of text (see, for example, Geertz [1988] 1989). Or, as Charles Briggs puts it, in "claiming to unveil the truth to convey information regarding some aspect of social reality, scholars construct the very Other they seek to describe" (1993, 387). On this reading, the search for "authenticity," and the way it is constructed or represented, is a political act.

In deference to this emerging argument, and a general uneasiness about attempts to represent the words of other people, in this book I have cut down on attempts to represent the paralinguistic features of the stories. Readers already know how oral storytellers sound when they take the floor (for at one time or another we have all been storytellers or audiences ourselves), so there is no need to go overboard trying to represent them. Moreover, if we overdo the effects, we risk unintentionally presenting the story-tellers in a light they would resent. So in this book I have simply aimed to present a *readable* text. I have used small capitals to show marked emphasis, and I have tidied the stories up a little bit by taking out "er's and um's" and minor false starts. Where breaks and false starts are important in signifying a speaker's hesitation or a wish to realign the sentence, however, I have left them in and sig-nified the break with a dash followed by a space (—). This looks a little odd, but it is the clearest way of representing the way speakers sometimes suddenly break off mid-sentence as if it is car-rying them along in the wrong direction.

I have omitted very little except where I have needed to quote extracts from a long narrative. In this case, I have indicated where the text is discontinuous by using an ellipsis in the usual way (. . .). I have never interfered with a speaker's grammar or lexis, and I have tried to follow what I judge the narrator's punctuation-intentions would be. This particularly affects cases where the narra-tor uses long strings of clauses loosely joined together by the word *and*. I have represented these as a single sentence, odd though it sometimes looks, because I feel that the presence of the word *and* indicates that the storyteller sees all this information as themati-cally linked (see Bennett 1990). On the other hand, *but* and *because* are sometimes capitalized. This occurs where I have judged, by following a speaker's tone, tempo, and intonation, that she intends to indicate the start of a new sentence. My observation is that these words are often used as disjunctions in informal oral sto-rytelling, and should not be confused with the same words when used as conjunctions.[1]

The narrator of each story or speaker of each bit of discourse is given at the end of the quotation; in the case of material from the Manchester research, the reader may find a little information about the storyteller in appendix 3. This information is not avail-able in the case of the Leicester research.

A typical story will look like this:

- I think yes! Because of my mother-in-law's experience.
  About three days before she died, she told me she was dying, and that her husband, my father-in-law, and

his sister, had been to see her and they told her that everything was perfectly all right, and— Oh, I was just flabbergasted, because she was the sort of person with no imagination WHATSOEVER. She couldn't have dreamt it up! She wasn't the type.

He died about ten months before her and the sister died about fourteen, fifteen months before. Oh, she was quite happy. She'd talked to them, you know.

She was quite relieved.

That was my own experience, because I'd be about twenty-eight. I hadn't come across anyone so SURE, and, had she been a very imaginative, chatty sort of person, probably I wouldn't have taken any notice, but she was ABSOLUTELY convinced. I mean, who am I to say that she didn't hear them, see them, or speak to them?

She was going to join them. It was eerie at the time, but as I've got older I've thought more about it, "Oh, yes! There must be something in it!" (Berenice*)

"Alas, Poor Ghost!"

Appendix 3

The Manchester Respondents

(Comprising eighty-seven women age 60–96, plus four women 40–60 years old whose stories are quoted [marked with *].)

pseudonym	marital status	age	domestic circumstances	(former) occupation
Abigail	married	70+	lives with husband	housewife
Ada	single	70+	lives alone	postmistress
Alice	married	60+	lives with husband	teacher
Alma	widowed	70+	lives alone	housewife
Annie	married	60+	lives with husband	housewife
Agnes	married	60+	lives with husband	housewife
Audrey	widowed	70+	lives alone	housewife
Beatie	widowed	70+	lives alone	housewife
Berenice*	married	40+	lives with husband	office worker
Bertha	married	70+	lives with husband	housewife
Bessie	widowed	70+	lives alone	housewife
Carrie	widowed	70+	lives alone	housewife
Catherine	single	70+	lives alone	unknown
Cecily	single	60+	lives alone	dressmaker
Clara	single	60+	lives with sister	abattoir owner
Clarice	widowed	70+	lives alone	housewife
Colette	married	60+	lives with husband	housewife
Constance	single	70+	lives alone	unknown
Cora	widowed	70+	lives alone	housewife

Dolly	no biographical details known			
Dora	single	70+	lives with friend	civil servant
Doris	married	60+	lives with husband	housewife
Doreen	no biographical details known			
Dorothy	widowed	80+	lives alone	housewife
Edie	widowed	70+	lives alone	businesswoman
Edna	single	80+	lives alone	unknown
Elisabeth	widowed	70+	lives alone	musician
Enid	single	70+	lives with sister	unknown
Ella	married	70+	lives with grandson	housewife
Evelyn	widowed	70+	lives alone	cleaner
Flo	widowed	80+	lives with daughter	housewife
Geraldine	single	60+	lives alone	teacher
Gert	widowed	70+	lives alone	housewife
Gladys	widowed	60+	lives alone	housewife
Gloria*	married	40+	lives with husband	dinner lady
Gwen	widowed	70+	lives alone	unknown
Harriet	widowed	80+	lives with daughter	housewife
Hilda	single	60+	lives with mother	psychologist
Inez	widowed	70+	lives with daughter	office worker
Iris	married	60+	lives with husband	housewife
Jane	no biographical details known			
Joan	married	70+	lives with husband	housewife
Joyce	widowed	60+	lives alone	housewife
Julia	married	60+	lives with husband	actress
Kate	no biographical details known			
Kathleen	widowed	70+	lives alone	housewife
Laura	no biographical details known			
Lavinia	single	60+	lives with sister	businesswoman
Lettie	married	60+	lives with husband	housewife
Lily	married	60+	lives with husband	housewife
Lydia	widowed	70+	lives with daughter	housewife
Mabel	single	70+	lives alone	businesswoman
Marjorie	no biographical details known			
Margaret	widowed	60+	lives alone	shopkeeper
Margot	single	60+	lives with sister	secretary
Mary	married	70+	lives with husband	housewife
Maud	widowed	60+	lives with son	businesswoman
Maura	widowed	70+	lives alone	housewife
May	married	80+	lives with husband	housewife
Meg	married	70+	lives with husband	housewife

"Alas, Poor Ghost!"

Molly*	married	40+	lives with husband	clerk
Nadine	widowed	70+	lives alone	housewife
Norah	widowed	60+	lives alone	shop assistant
Norma	widowed	70+	lives alone	housewife
Olive	married	60+	lives with husband	housewife
Patricia	married	70+	lives with husband	housewife
Paula	married	60+	lives with husband	housewife
Phyllis	single	70+	lives alone	unknown
Polly	widowed	70+	lives alone	teacher
Queenie	single	70+	lives alone	businesswoman
Rachel	widowed	80+	lives alone	housewife
Renee	married	70+	lives with husband	housewife
Rina	married	70+	lives with husband	counselor
Rita	widowed	70+	lives alone	housewife
Rose	married	60+	lives with husband	bookmaker
Ruth	widowed	70+	lives with son	housewife
Sarah	widowed	60+	lives alone	housewife
Stella	married	70+	lives with husband	housewife
Susan	widowed	70+	lives alone	housewife
Sylvia*	single	40+	lives with mother	solicitor's clerk
Thomasine	widowed	60+	lives alone	housewife
Thora	married	80+	lives with husband	housewife
Trixie	widowed	70+	lives alone	housewife
Una	widowed	60+	lives alone	shopkeeper
Valerie	married	60+	lives with husband	housewife
Vanessa	widowed	80+	lives alone	housewife
Vera	single	70+	lives alone	businesswoman
Violet	married	60+	lives with husband	housewife
Winifred	widowed	60+	lives with daughter	housewife
Zena	widowed	70+	lives with brother	housewife
Zillah	widowed	70+	lives alone	housewife

Appendix 4

Linguistic Clues to Belief and Disbelief

Convinced belief
 "I FIRMLY believe"
 "I do believe in that"
 "Yes, oh yes"
 "Without question"
 "I've PROOF of that"
 prompt or precipitate reply
Some belief
 "Not REALLY, but"
 "Possibly there is something IN that"
 "I THINK there COULD be"
 "I don't say I BELIEVE it, but"
Don't know
 "I don't know"
 "I get a bit mixed up about that"
 hesitation unaccompanied by embarrassment
Some scepticism
 "I don't take any notice of that kind of thing"
 "I don't think so, REALLY"
Convinced disbelief
 "I don't believe in that"
 "I just don't SEE"
 laughter

grimaces
headshakes
(intonation) absence of stress on verbs expressing knowl-
              edge, belief, or understanding; stress placed on
              word for *object* of knowledge

Appendix 5

Word Lists Showing
Story Patterns in Memorates

T he figures in parentheses represent the number of times a given word is used in memorates on the subject of visitations. Note, though, that some stories will feature many of the words listed in each table, others few or none.

Where?

indoors	*outdoors*
house (15)	garden (1)
bedroom (14)	lane (1)
room (5)	
kitchen (1)	
workplace (1)	

When?

hour	*frequency invariable*	*frequency common*	*frequency infrequent*	*frequency specific*
night (11)	always(10)	many times (1)	sometimes (2)	once (9)
day (8)	whenever(1)	several times (1)	occasionally (1)	when (5)
morning (1)	every time(1)	often (1)		ago (3)
				after (3)
				before (2)

In what circumstances?

asleep	untroubled	mental distress	physical distress
dreaming (2)	wide awake (4)	searching (3)	dying (5)
		low (2)	tired (2)
		muddled (2)	ill (4)
		uncertain (1)	delirious (1)
		shocked (1)	going through the
		praying (1)	crisis (1)
		praying (1)	

What ?

approach	communication	perception	cognition	action
come (8)	tell (8)	see (12)	feel (16)	help (3)
meet (4)	say (8)	touch (4)	think (4)	look at (3)
go (1)	cough (2)	hear (3)	imagine (3)	hold (1)
open (door) (1)	listen (1)	smell (1)	know (2)	give (1)
stand (1)	talk (1)	experience (1)		rub (1)
walk (1)	ask (1)			bend (over) (1)
pass (1)	reassure (1)			tuck up (1)
	show (1)			smile (1)
	call (1)			hide (1)
	warn (1)			shake (1)
	remind (1)			wake (1)
	speak (1)			break (1)

"Alas, Poor Ghost!"

Who?

relative
parent (20)
husband (9)
child (5)
grandparent(3)
aunt (1)
family (1)

human
lady (3)
someone (3)
people (2)
they (2)
she (2)

spiritual
presence (8)
message (3)
apparition (1)
spirit (1)

disembodied
voice (3)
face (1)
something (1)

animal
cat (1)

inanimate
smoke (1)
flowers (1)

How?

explicit
alive (15)
is (15)
there (7)
plainly (5)
strongly (4)
distinctly (3)
true (3)
clearly (2)

vague
as though (8)
sort of (2)
like (2)
somehow (1)
in a way (1)
unconsciously (1)

described as being
in white (1)
in uniform (1)
with his arms up (1)
cross (1)
unhappy (1)
like a grey shadow (1)

Where?

preposition	internal	external
to (8)	in my brain (1)	in the bedroom (4)
in (8)	in my vision (1)	there (3)
with (4)	in my head (1)	in the house (1)
in front of (4)	in my dream (1)	in the room (1)
before (3)		near (1)
at (3)		
by (3)		
beside (2)		
back (2)		
around (2)		
up (1)		
through(1)		
round (1)		

"Alas, Poor Ghost!"

Notes

1. Comparable figures were obtained from the group of younger women I interviewed. Fifty-seven percent believed in some sort of contact with the family dead; 57 percent believed in hauntings or "unhappy" houses. It is not possible, of course, to make too much of these figures given the small number of younger respondents, but it does allow me occasionally to illustrate my discussion with one of their stories. See appendix 3 and chapter 2, note 4.

2. For a folkloric study of dreams and foreknowledge, see Kaivola-Bregenhøj 1990. It may be significant, and it certainly is interesting, to observe that a larger number of younger women believed in "premonitions" than older ones, but fewer younger ones believed in telepathy. Figures for "premonitions" were 83 percent among 40–60-year-olds, and 77 percent among the over-sixties; figures for "telepathy" were 55 percent among the younger group, 70 percent among the older group.

3. In all extracts from the Manchester interviews, respondents are identified by a pseudonym. Brief biographical details of each one may be found by consulting appendix 3.

4. For transcription conventions used throughout this book, see the discussion in appendix 2.

5. This is Lang's own description of himself. See "Protest of a Psycho-Folklorist" (Lang 1895).

CHAPTER 2

1. The word list technique has been successfully used by other researchers interested in folk belief. Noel Williams, for example,

used the method to show the contexts and implications of the word "fairy" in texts from 1320 to 1829 (Williams 1983), and William Lynwood Montell used it (perhaps less rigorously but no less usefully) to summarize the essential characteristics of ghosts as they appear in his wonderful story compilation *Ghosts along the Cumberland* ([1975] 1987, 90–94).

2. For the transcription conventions used throughout this book, see appendix 2.

3. For a discussion of the way hauntings have got attached to the idea of unnatural deaths see "The Vanishing Hitchhiker" stories in chapter 5.

4. Unless otherwise stated, all illustrative material in chapters 1, 2, and 4 is taken from the eighty-seven women selected for the Manchester study. Very occasionally, as here, stories told by one of the slightly younger women I interviewed have been used, but only on subjects where I found no significant divergence between older and younger women's viewpoints (see chapter 1, note 1). At all times this is noted by placing an asterisk after the name. Details of all the respondents are given in appendix 3.

5. A similar experience is reported by clinical psychologist Michael F. Hoyt as his "case 3" (1980–81, 107–8).

6. In this respect it is interesting to observe that two stories may actually provide an example of personal experience becoming integrated into community folklore and being changed to fit it better. In the first of the stories below, Ella, a married woman in her seventies, tells the story about the "lady in white." In the second one, Ruth, a widow in her seventies, repeats the experience of a fellow Guild member (the Methodist Guild, a study and discussion group) in order to back up her own point of view. As both were members of the local Methodist church, was Ella the Guild member Ruth speaks of, and is this the story that she was told? If it is not the same story, then how can one account for the strong similarities in the way the child's illness is described? If it *is* the same story, note that the experience has been changed to accommodate a mother as the agent of healing rather than an anonymous lady in white, and the way the experience has been shaped by interpretations and beliefs which are not present in the original.

- My daughter, too, she was very ill for a long time. She was only about four I think. She'd be about seven, and she was very ill. She has had a lot of illness, but she was very ill at this time. She'd had measles very badly and was in a bad way actually, and I looked after, was nursing her at home, and she says a lady in white came to see her and told her to get better.

Now I don't know. I mean she was seven then. But from then on, funnily enough, she got better. But she says, she often talks about it even now, the lady in white was standing by her in the bedroom. Hard to believe, isn't it really? I don't know, I mean she might have been delirious or something, I don't know. But she always said, "There was a lady in white came to see me when I had measles." When she was younger she used to say.

- It is my belief, I believe in life after death, you see. I don't know, of course. None of us know how this is going to be, but I think that the spirit of those who've gone, it's there! Now if ever perhaps you might get yourself into a situation where the spirit is going to help you sometime, I think it might be possible. I think it's possible.

  One of our Guild members was saying—she came to see me after Charlotte died—and she said she always remembers when her daughter was very, very young, I think it was measles she had, but she had it very badly, and she was delirious with it, and she had to go out of the room, and she was very very worried, and she suddenly got the feeling that her mother who had died had sort of reassured her that the child would be all right while she was out of the room and she said, when she came back this child was calm and quiet as ever! She thought—she just felt her mother was present, helping her. Of course, that was I don't know what. She didn't—she doesn't go to church very regularly, but she does believe.

7. Compare this account from Geoffrey Gorer:

    If I'd got worries I used to take them to her, you see; and I feel that I should get some sign from her somehow that puts me on the right track. . . . I still feel that if I had any worries and I prayed for help and guidance from her, I would get it (1977, 100).

Chapter 3

1. Pronounced "Lester."
2. Throughout this chapter, the Leicester respondents are referred to as Mrs. A, B, C and so on through to Mrs. T. No further information is given lest the respondents be identified.
3. The interviewer omitted to ask two women this question.
4. Like many informal oral storytellers, the Leicester widows do not prioritize time and sequence in their narratives, but group events together by theme, circling round images and happenings which are central to their perception of the relevance and meaning of the events they are describing (as we shall see in chapter 4). The interviewer was as much audience as questioner so she could not keep interrupting to ask the speaker to specify the time lapse. Again, the fact that certain types of emotions and experiences are not mentioned in the narratives does not mean that they were outside the narrators' experiences; it might simply mean that they had forgotten them or expressed them in a way which the listener or reader failed to understand the significance of.
5. Or maybe to keep their minds off their fear? One possible interpretation of their fear of going to bed, their reluctance to stay in the house, and their "flight into activity" is that there is some degree of fear of the dead in modern society. The women may be desperate to have their husbands back alive, but fearful that they will come back to them dead.
6. It is possible that there are socioeconomic dimensions to this criterion, in terms of the desire that the widow should not be a "burden" on the state or family. For a discussion of these issues, see Prosterman 1996, 190–93.
7. One, to us, very strange effect of the stress currently laid on the role of the professional attendant can be seen in a recent discussion by Robert Weiss (1993), in which he lists "four relational bonds," the severance of which results in typical grief reactions. These are pair bonds, parental bonds, "persistence of childhood attachment into adulthood" (by which he means the bond adult children feel for their parents, "an unusual development" he says), and the "transference" bond patients sometimes form with their therapists. Thus he expects adult children to be only "briefly bereft" after the death of a parent but to be potentially seriously

distressed by the loss of a therapist. Extraordinary! (see Weiss 1993, 274–76).

8. See, for example, Schulz 1978, 137; Kastenbaum 1981, 223–24; Sanders 1989, 70–71; Shuchter and Zisook 1993, 34–35; Littlewood 1992, 47; Bowling and Cartwright 1982, 141; and Parkes 1986, 70.

9. The Phillips quotation comes from *Ring of Truth* (Phillips 1967, 89–90).

10. Interestingly, C. S. Lewis records feeling the sense of his wife's presence at the end of his account of his own bereavement, *A Grief Observed* (1961).

11. This heartbreaking account is a clear example of the "searching" process discussed by Bowlby (1961). A well-known literary account of this phenomenon, combined with the sleeplessness and restlessness so often noted in the bereavement literature, can be found in the "Dark House" sequence of Tennyson's *In Memoriam* (1850).

> Dark house, by which once more I stand
> Here in the long, unlovely street,
> Doors, where my heart was used to beat
> So quickly, waiting for a hand,
>
> A hand that can be clasp'd no more—
> Behold me, for I cannot sleep,
> And like a guilty thing I creep
> At earliest morning to the door.
>
> He is not here; but far away
> The noise of life begins again,
> And ghastly thro' the drizzling rain
> On the bald street breaks the blank day.
> (Leeson 1980, 365)

12. These experiences, particularly the frightening one, sound very like the classic ghosts who get into bed with the living or disturb the bedclothes. The feeling that someone is in bed with one deserves a full-scale Huffordesque treatment.

13. David Hufford is undoubtedly right when he says that a writer's choice between the terms "vision" and "hallucination" are accurate guides to their acceptance or lack of acceptance of the possibility of

the supernatural: "The choice between them is determined by the speaker's evaluation of the alleged perceiver's correctness or error" (Hufford 1985, 89).

Chapter 4

1. Richard Bauman calls this "keying" the discourse for performance, R. E. Longacre calls it creating an "aperture" for a story. Gary Butler calls it "framing in" to a narrative (Bauman 1977, 15–24, esp. 19–21; Longacre 1976, 214; Butler 1990, 108). I shall use Longacre's neutral term throughout. For a discussion of tense change as a way of signalling the onset of narrative, see Jakobson 1971.

2. Labov and Waletsky call this a "coda"; Longacre calls it a "closure"; Janet Langlois calls it a "metagloss" (Labov and Waletsky 1967; Longacre 1976, 214; Langlois 1978, 149). Again, I prefer Longacre's term because it commits the analyst to less comment about its interpretative significance.

3. This is not the only account of a supernatural experience while cleaning teeth. Douglas Davies notes that one of his respondents sensed the presence of her stepmother while cleaning her teeth (1997, 160).

Chapter 5

1. There are two rather different accounts of ghost traditions in Grose's *Provincial Glossary*, one of which seems to me to be plainly contemporary country superstition; the other is the one quoted here. In *Traditions of Belief* I discussed my reasons for thinking this passage was based on the polemical writing of the late seventeenth century (see Bennett 1987, 182–83).

Appendix 1

1. The name "Cruse," literally a jar or pot, comes from a biblical reference. See 1 Kings 17:10–16, where the prophet Elijah demands bread and water from a starving widow woman. She has only a little meal in the bottom of a barrel and a drop of oil in a cruse but makes a little cake to give him. She is rewarded by the barrel never being used up and the cruse always containing oil.

2.   Twenty interviews were undertaken, but one respondent was plainly ill, so her interview was not used for research purposes.

Appendix 2

1.   To standardize the presentation of stories in this book, I have repunctuated material taken from the Leicester study in accordance with these principles.

References Cited

Atwater, P. M. H. 1988. *Coming Back to Life: The After Effects of the Near-Death Experience*. New York: Ballantine Book.

Aubrey, John. 1696. *Miscellanies*. London: Edward Castle.

Averill, James R., and Elma P. Nunley. 1993. "Grief as an Emotion and as a Disease: A Social-Constructionist Perspective." In *Handbook of Bereavement: Theory, Research, and Intervention*, ed. M. S. Stroebe, W. Stroebe, and R. O. Hansson. Cambridge: Cambridge University Press.

Ballard, Linda-May. 1981. "Before Death and Beyond—A Preliminary Survey of Death and Ghost Traditions with Particular Reference to Ulster." In *The Folklore of Ghosts*, ed. Hilda R. Ellis Davidson and W. M. S. Russell. Mistletoe Series. Bury St Edmunds: D. S. Brewer for the Folklore Society.

Basford, T. K. 1990. *Near-Death Experiences: An Annotated Bibliography*. London and New York: Garland.

Bauman, Richard. 1977. *Verbal Art as Performance*. Prospect Heights, Illinois: Waveland Press.

———. 1986. *Story, Performance, and Event: Contextual Studies in Oral Narrative*. Cambridge: Cambridge University Press.

Baxter, Richard. [1691] 1840. *The Certainty of the World of Spirits Fully Evinced, to Which Is Added "The Wonders of the Invisible World" by Cotton Mather*. Reprint, London: H. Howell.

Beardsley, Richard K., and Rosalie Hankey. 1942. "The Vanishing Hitchhiker." *California Folklore Quarterly* 1:303–35.

Beardsley, Richard K., and Rosalie Hankey. 1943. "A History of the Vanishing Hitchhiker." *California Folklore Quarterly* 2:13–25.

Beaumont, John. 1705. *An Historical, Physiological, and Theological Treatise of Spirits, Apparitions, Witchcrafts, and Other Magical Practices*. London: D. Browne.

Bennett, Gillian. 1984. "The Phantom Hitchhiker: Neither Modern, Urban, nor Legend?" In *Perspectives on Contemporary Legend: Proceedings of the Conference on Contemporary Legend, Sheffield, July 1982*, ed. Paul Smith. CECTAL Conference Papers Series. Sheffield: CECTAL.

——. 1986. "Narrative as Expository Discourse." *Journal of American Folklore* 99:415–34.

——. 1987. *Traditions of Belief: Women and the Supernatural*. Harmondsworth: Pelican.

——. 1989a. "'Belief Stories': The Forgotten Genre." *Western Folklore* 48:289–311.

——. 1989b. "Playful Chaos: Anatomy of a Storytelling Session." In *The Questing Beast: Perspectives on Contemporary Legend*, vol. 4, ed. Gillian Bennett and Paul Smith. Sheffield: Sheffield Academic Press.

——. 1990. "'And . . .': Controlling the Argument, Controlling the Audience." *Fabula* 31:78–87.

——. 1993. "The Color of Saying: Contemporary Legend as Folktale." *Southern Folklore* 50:19–32.

——. 1995. "'If I Knew You Were Coming I'd Have Baked a Cake': The Folklore of Foreknowledge in a Neighborhood Group." In *Out of the Ordinary: Folklore and the Supernatural*, ed. Barbara Walker. Logan: Utah State University Press.

——. 1997. "The Vanishing Hitchhiker and the Bad Death." Paper presented at the 3rd conference on the social aspects of death and dying, University of Sussex.

——. 1998. "The Vanishing Hitchhiker at Fifty-Five." *Western Folklore* 57:1–17.

Bennett, Gillian, and Paul Smith. 1993. *Contemporary Legend: A Folklore Bibliography*. New York: Garland.

Bennett, K. M. 1996. "A Longitudinal Study of Wellbeing in Widowed Women." *International Journal of Geriatric Psychiatry* 11:1005–10.

——. 1998. "Longitudinal Changes in Mental and Physical Health among Elderly Recently Widowed Men." *Mortality* 3:265–74.

Bennett, K. M., and K. Morgan. 1992. "Health, Social Functioning, and Marital Status: Stability and Change among Elderly Recently Widowed Women." *International Journal of Geriatric Psychiatry* 7:813–17.

Benveniste, E. 1966. *Problèmes de linguistique générale*. Paris: Gallimard.

Blauner, Robert. 1966. "Death and Social Structure." *Psychiatry* 29:378–94.

Bourne, Henry. [1725] 1977. *Antiquitates Vulgares, or The Antiquities of the Common People*. Reprint, New York: Arno Press.

Bovet, Richard. [1684] 1951. *Pandaemonium, or The Devil's Cloister*. Reprint, Aldington, Kent: Hand and Flower Press.

Bowlby, John. 1961. "Processes of Mourning." *International Journal of Psychoanalysis* 42:317–40.

Bowling, Ann, and Ann Cartwright. 1982. *Life after a Death: A Study of the Elderly Widowed*. London and New York: Tavistock Publications.

Brand, John. 1777. *Observations on Popular Antiquities; including the whole of Mr Bourne's Antiquitates Vulgares, with Addenda to every chapter of that work: As also an Appendix, containing such Articles as have been omitted by that Author*. Newcastle-upon-Tyne: J. Johnson.

Briggs, Charles L. 1993. "Metadiscursive Practices and Scholarly Authority in Folkloristics." *Journal of American Folklore* 106:387–434.

Browne, Ray B. 1976. *"A Night with the Hants" and Other Alabama Folk Experiences*. Bowling Green: University Popular Press.

Brunvand, Jan Harold. 1986. *The Mexican Pet: More "New" Urban Legends and Some Old Favorites*. New York and London: W. W. Norton.

Burne, Charlotte. 1883. *Shropshire Folklore: A Sheaf of Gleanings from the Notebooks of Georgina F. Jackson*. London: Trench Trübner.

Burrison, John A., ed. 1989. *Storytellers: Folktales and Legends from the South*. Athens and London: University of Georgia Press.

Butler, Gary R. 1990. *Saying Isn't Believing: Conversation, Narrative, and the Discourse of Belief in a French Newfoundland Community*. St John's: ISER, Memorial University of Newfoundland.

Campion-Vincent, Véronique, and Jean-Bruno Renard. 1992. *Légendes urbaines: Rumeurs d'aujourd'hui*. Paris: Payot.

Charmaz, K. 1980. *The Social Reality of Death*. Reading, Massachusetts: Addison-Wesley.

Clodd, Edward. 1895a. "Presidential Address." *Folk-Lore* 6:54–81.

———. 1895b. "A Reply to the Foregoing 'Protest.'" *Folk-Lore* 6:248–58.

———. 1896. "Presidential Address." *Folk-Lore* 7:35–60.

Cohan, Steven, and Linda M. Shires. 1988. *Telling Stories: A Theoretical Analysis of Narrative Fiction*. New York and London: Routledge.

Crowe, Mrs Catherine. 1848. *The Night-Side of Nature, or Ghosts and Ghost-Seers*. London: Routledge.

Cunningham, Keith. 1979. "The Vanishing Hitchhiker in Arizona— Almost." *Southwest Folklore* 3:46–50.

Danielson, Larry. 1979. "Toward the Analysis of Vernacular Texts: The Supernatural Narrative in Oral and Popular Print Sources." *Journal of the Folklore Institute* 16:130–54.

———. 1983. "Paranormal Narratives in the American Vernacular." In *The Occult in America*, ed. Howard Kerr and Charles L. Crow. Urbana and Chicago: University of Chicago Press.

Davies, Douglas J. 1997. *Death, Ritual, and Belief: The Rhetoric of Funerary Rites*. London and Washington: Cassell.

Davies, Douglas, and Alastair Shaw. 1995. *Reusing Old Graves: A Report on Popular British Attitudes*. Crayford, Kent: Shaw and Sons.

Davies, D. J., C. Watkins, and M. Winter. 1991. *Church and Religion in Rural England*. Edinburgh: T. and T. Clark.

Defoe, Daniel [Andrew Moreton, pseud.]. 1729. *The Secrets of the Invisible World Disclos'd*. London: J. Clarke, A. Millar, C. Rivington and J. Green.

Dégh, Linda. 1971. "The 'Belief Legend' in Modern Society: Form, Function, and Relationship to Other Genres." In *American Folk Legend: A Symposium*, ed. Wayland D. Hand. Berkeley, Los Angeles, and London: University of California Press.

———. 1996. "What Is a Belief Legend?" *Folklore* 107:33–46.

Dégh, Linda, and Andrew Vázsonyi. 1971. "Legend and Belief." *Genre* 4:281–304.

———. 1973. "The Dialectics of Legend." Folklore Preprints Series, no. 6. Bloomington, Indiana.

———. 1974. "The Memorate and the Proto-memorate." *Journal of American Folklore* 87:225–39.

———. 1975. "The Hypothesis of Multi-conduit Transmission in Folklore." In *Folklore: Performance and Communications*, ed. Dan Ben Amos and Kenneth Goldstein. The Hague: Mouton.

Dickenson, Donna, and Malcolm Johnson, eds. 1993. *Death, Dying, and Bereavement*. London, Newbury Park (California), and New Delhi: Sage Publications in association with the Open University.

Dijk, Teun van. 1974–75. "Action, Action-Description, and Narrative." *New Literary History* 6:273–94.

Dodson, Ruth. 1943. "The Ghost Nun." In *Backwoods to Border*, ed. Mody C. Boatright and Donald Day. Publications of the Texas Folklore Society. Dallas: Southern Methodist University Press.

Dorson, Richard M. 1964. *Buying the Wind: Regional Folklore in the United States*. Chicago: Chicago University Press.

———. 1968a. *The British Folklorists: A History*. London: Routledge and Kegan Paul.

———. 1968b. *Peasant Customs and Savage Myths: Selections from the British Folklorists*. 2 vols. London and Chicago: Routledge and Kegan Paul and the University of Chicago Press.

Dover Wilson, John. 1959. *What Happens in Hamlet*. Cambridge: Cambridge University Press.

Dumerchat, Frédéric. 1990. "Les auto-stoppeurs fantômes: Des récits légendaires contemporains." *Communications* 52:249–81.

Dupi, B. 1982. "La dame blanche ou quand l'autostoppeuse se volatalise." *Lumières dans la Nuit* (March/April).

Easlea, Brian. 1980. *Witchhunting, Magic, and the New Philosophy*. Brighton: Harvester.

Edgerton, William B. 1968. "The Ghost in Search of Help for a Dying Man." *Journal of the Folklore Institute* 5:31–41.

Ellis, Bill. 1987. "Why Are Verbatim Transcripts of Legends Necessary?" In *Perspectives on Contemporary Legend*, vol. 2, ed. Gillian Bennett, Paul Smith, and J. D. A. Widdowson. CECTAL Conference Papers Series. Sheffield: Sheffield Academic Press/CECTAL.

Fine, Elizabeth C. [1984] 1994. *The Folklore Text: From Performance to Print*. Reprint, Bloomington: Indiana University Press.

Finucane, R. C. 1982. *Appearances of the Dead: A Cultural History of Ghosts*. London: Junction Books.

Fish, Lydia M. 1976. "Jesus on the Thruway: The Vanishing Hitchhiker Strikes Again." *Indiana Folklore* 9:5–13.

Fonda, Jesse. 1977. "I Met the Real Phantom Hitchhiker" *Fate* 30:55–57.

Footman, Els Ballhausen. 1998. "The Loss Adjusters." *Mortality* 3:291–95.

Gaudet, Marcia. 1992. "Miss Jane and Personal Experience Narrative." *Western Folklore* 51:23–32.

Geertz, Clifford. [1988] 1989. *Works and Lives: The Anthropologist as Author*. Reprint, Cambridge: Polity Press.

Giraud, S. Louis. 1927. *True Ghost Stories Told by Readers of the "Daily News."* London: Fleetgate Publications, Daily News Book Department.

Glanvil, Joseph. 1681. *Sadducismus Triumphatus*. London: Thomas Newcombe.

Glassie, Henry. 1982. *Passing the Time in Balleymenone: Culture and History of an Ulster Community*. Philadelphia: University of Pennsylvania Press.

Glazer, Mark. 1986. "The Mexican-American Legend in the Rio Grande Valley: An Overview." *Borderlands* 10:143–60.

———. 1987. "The Cultural Adaptation of a Rumour Legend: 'The Boyfriend's Death' in South Texas." In *Perspectives on Contemporary Legend*, vol. 2, ed. Gillian Bennett, Paul Smith, and J. D. A. Widdowson. CECTAL Conference Papers Series. Sheffield: Sheffield Academic Press/CECTAL.

Glick, Ira O., Robert S. Weiss, and Colin Murray Parkes. 1974. *The First Year of Bereavement*. New York and London: John Wiley and Sons.

Goin, M. K., R. W. Burgoyne, and J. M. Goin. 1979. "Timeless Attachment to a Dead Relative." *American Journal of Psychiatry* 136:988–89.

Goldsmith, Oliver (attributed). 1742. *The Mystery Revealed: containing a series of transactions and authentic testimonials respecting the supposed Cock Lane Ghost*. London: n.p.

Gorer, Geoffrey. 1955. *Exploring English Character*. London: Cresset Press.

———. [1965] 1977. *Death, Grief, and Mourning*. Reprint, New York: Arno.

Goss, Michael. 1982. "Taken for a Ride?" *The Unexplained* 8:1706–9.

———. 1984. *The Evidence for Phantom Hitch-Hikers: An Objective Survey of the Phantom Hitch-Hiker Phenomenon in All Its Manifestations*. Wellingborough: Aquarian Press in conjunction with ASSAP, the Association for the Scientific Study of Anomalous Phenomena.

———. 1986. "The Hitch-Hiker on Public Transport." *Magonia* 22:3–6, 8.

Greeley, Andrew M. 1975. *The Sociology of the Paranormal: A Reconnaissance*. London and Beverley Hills: Sage.

Green, Celia, and Charles McCreery. 1975. *Apparitions*. London: Hamish Hamilton.

Greyson, B., and C. P. Flynn, eds. 1984. *The Near-Death Experience: Problems, Prospects, Perspectives*. Springfield, Illinois: Charles C. Thomas.

Grimes, J. E. 1972. "Outlines and Overlays." *Language* 48:513–24.

———. 1975. *Thread of Discourse*. Jannua Linguarum, series minor. The Hague: Mouton.

Grose, Francis. [1787] 1790. *A Provincial Glossary with a Collection of Local Proverbs and Popular Superstitions*. Reprint, London: S. Hooper.

"Alas, Poor Ghost!"

Halpert, Herbert, and J. D. A. Widdowson. 1984. "Folk-Narrative Performance and Tape Transcription: Theory vs Practice." In *Papers 1: The 8th Congress for the International Society for Folk Narrative Research*, ed. Reimund Kvideland and Torunn Selberg. Bergen.

———. 1996. *Folktales of Newfoundland: The Resilience of the Oral Tradition*. New York: Garland.

Hand, Wayland D. 1976. "Folk Belief and Superstition: A Crucial Field of Folklore Long Neglected." In *Folklore Today: A Festschrift for Richard M. Dorson*, ed. Linda Dégh, Henry Glassie, and Felix J. Oinas. Bloomington: Indiana University Press.

Hankey, Rosalie. 1942. "California Ghosts." *California Folklore Quarterly* 1:155–77.

Hansson, Robert O., Jacqueline H. Remondet, and Marlene Galusha. 1993. "Old Age and Widowhood: Issues of Personal Control and Independence." In *Handbook of Bereavement: Theory, Research, and Intervention*, ed. M. S. Stroebe, W. Stroebe, and R. O. Hansson. Cambridge: Cambridge University Press.

Hare, Augustus. [1896] 1986. *The Story of My Life*. 6 vols. Reprint, London: George Allen.

Harpur, T. 1991. *Life after Death*. Toronto: McLelland and Stewart.

Harrold, Francis B., and Raymond A. Eve. 1986. "Noah's Ark and Ancient Astronauts: Pseudoscientific Beliefs about the Past among a Sample of College Students." *Skeptical Inquirer* 11:61–75.

Heyman, Dorothy K., and Daniel T. Gianturco. 1973. "Long-Term Adaptation by the Elderly to Bereavement." *Journal of Gerontology* 28:359–62.

Holck, Frederick H. 1978–79. "Life Revisited (Parallels in Death Experiences)." *Omega* 9:1–11.

Honko, Lauri. 1964. "Memorates and the Study of Folk Beliefs." *Journal of the Folklore Institute* 1:5–19.

Hoyt, Michael F. 1980–81. "Clinical Notes Regarding the Experience of 'Presences' in Mourning." *Omega* 11:105–11.

Hufford, David J. 1976. "A New Approach to the Old Hag." In *American Folk Medicine*, ed. Wayland D. Hand. Berkeley, Los Angeles, and London: University of California Press.

———. 1977. "Ambiguity and the Rhetoric of Belief." *Keystone Folklore* 21:11–24.

———. 1982a. *The Terror That Comes in the Night*. Philadelphia: University of Pennsylvania Press.

———. 1982b. "Traditions of Disbelief." *New York Folklore* 8:47–55.

————. 1985. "Commentary" to *And the World Was Flooded with Light* by Genevive Foster. Pittsburgh: University of Pittsburg Press.

————. 1992. Commentary to "Paranormal Experiences in the General Population." *Journal of Nervous and Mental Disease* 108:362–68.

Hunt, Robert. 1865. *Popular Romances of the West of England, or The Drolls, Traditions, and Superstitions of Old Cornwall.* 2 vols. London: John Camden Hotton.

Hutchinson, Francis [Bishop of Down and Connor]. 1720. *An Historical Essay Concerning Witchcraft with observations tending to confute the vulgar errors about that point. And also two sermons; one in proof of the Christian religion; the other concerning good and evil angels.* 2d ed. London: R. Knaplock and D. Midwinter.

Hymes, Dell. 1972. "Models of the Interaction of Language and Social Life." In *Directions in Sociolinguistics: The Ethnography of Communication,* ed. J. J. Gumperz and Dell Hymes. New York: Holt, Rinehart and Winston.

————. 1981. *"In Vain I Tried to Tell You": Studies in Native American Ethnopoetics.* Philadelphia: University of Pennsylvania Press.

Ingram, John J. 1884. *The Haunted Houses and Family Traditions of Great Britain.* London: W. H. Allen.

Ironside, Virginia. 1996. *"You'll Get Over It": Coping with Bereavement.* London: Hamish Hamilton.

Jaffé, Aniela. [1957] 1979. *Apparitions: An Archetypal Approach to Death, Dreams, and Ghosts.* Translation of *Geistererscheinungen und Vorzeichen.* Reprint, Irving, Texas: Spring Publications University of Dallas.

Jahoda, Gustav. 1969. *The Psychology of Superstition.* London: Allen Lane.

Jakobson, Roman. 1971. "Shifters, Verbal Categories, and the Russian Verb." Chap. in *Roman Jakobson: Selected Writings,* vol. 2. The Hague and Paris: Mouton.

Jones, Louis C. 1944a. "The Ghosts of New York." *Journal of American Folklore* 57:237–54.

————. 1944b. "Hitchhiking Ghosts in New York." *California Folklore Quarterly* 3:284–91.

————. 1959. *Things That Go Bump in the Night.* New York: Hill and Wang.

Jung, Carl Gustav. 1964. "The Psychological Foundation of Belief in Spirits." In *Collected Works,* vol. 8. London: Routledge and Kegan Paul.

Kaivola-Bregenhøj, Annikki. 1990. "From Dream to Interpretation." *International Folklore Review* 7:87–96.

Kalish, Richard A., and David K. Reynolds. 1973. "Phenomenological Reality and Post-death Contact." *Journal for the Scientific Study of Religion* 12:209–21.

Kakrup, Helen. 1982. *"Coventional Religion and Common Religion in Leeds."* *Interview Schedule: Basic Frequencies by Question.* Religious Research Papers, vol. 12. Leeds: University of Leeds, Department of Sociology.

Kastenbaum, Robert J. 1981. *Death, Society, and Human Experience.* St. Louis, Toronto, and London: C. V. Moseby.

Knierim, Volker. 1985. "Auto, Fremde, Tod: Automobile und Reisen in zeitgenössischen deutschsprachigen Sensationserzählungen." *Fabula* 26:230–44.

Kübler-Ross, Elisabeth. 1970. *On Death and Dying.* London: Tavistock.

Labov, William, and Joshua Waletsky. 1967. "Narrative Analysis: Oral Versions of Personal Experience." In *Essays on the Visual and Verbal Arts*, ed. June Helm. Seattle: University of Washington Press.

Lang, Andrew. 1894. *Cock Lane and Common-Sense.* London: Longman's.

———. 1895. "Protest of a Psycho-Folklorist." *Folk-Lore* 6:236–48.

———. 1897. *Dreams and Ghosts.* London: Longman's.

Langlois, Janet. 1978. "Belle Gunness, the Lady Bluebeard: Community Legend as Metaphor." *Journal of Folklore Research* 15:147–60.

Lavater, Lewes (Ludowig). [1572] 1929. *Of Ghosts and Spirits Walking by Night.* Reprint, Oxford: The Shakespearian Association at the University Press.

Lea, H. C. 1957. *Materials toward a History of Witchcraft.* New York and London: Thomas Yoseloff.

Leather, Ella Mary. 1912. *The Folk-Lore of Herefordshire.* Hereford and London: Jakeman & Carver/Sidgwick and Jackson.

Le Loyer, Pierre. [1586] 1605. *A Treatise of Spectres.* Trans. Z. Jones. London: n.p.

Leeson, Edward (compiler). 1980. *The New Golden Treasury of English Verse.* London: Macmillan.

Lewes, Mary L. 1911. *Stranger Than Fiction.* London: William Rider and Son.

Lewis, C. S. 1961. *A Grief Observed.* London: Faber.

Lieberman, M. A. 1993. "Counseling and Therapy of the Bereaved." In *Handbook of Bereavement: Theory, Research, and Intervention*, ed. M. S. Stroebe, W. Stroebe, and R. O. Hansson. Cambridge: Cambridge University Press.

Lindemann, Erich. 1944. "Symptomatology and Management of Acute Grief." *American Journal of Psychiatry* 101:141–48.

Littlewood, Jane. 1992. *Aspects of Grief: Bereavement in Adult Life.* London and New York: Routledge.

Longacre, R. E. 1976. *An Anatomy of Speech Notions.* Lisse: Peter de Ridder Press.

Lopata, Helena Znaniecka. 1996. *Current Widowhood: Myths and Realities.* London and New Delhi: Sage.

Luomala, Katharine. 1972. "Disintegration and Regeneration, the Hawaiian Phantom Hitchhiker Legend." *Fabula* 13:20–59.

Marris, Peter. 1958. *Widows and Their Families.* London: Routledge and Kegan Paul.

———. 1974. *Loss and Change.* London: Routledge and Kegan Paul.

Martin, David. 1967. *A Sociology of English Religion.* London: Heineman.

McEntire, Dee L. 1992. "Erotic Storytelling: Sexual Experience and Fantasy Letters in Forum Magazine." *Western Folklore* 51:81–96.

Middleton, W., B. Raphael, N. Martinek, and V. Misso. 1993. "Pathological Grief Reactions." In *Handbook of Bereavement: Theory, Research, and Intervention,* ed. M. S. Stroebe, W. Stroebe, and R. O. Hansson. Cambridge: Cambridge University Press.

Mitchell, Roger. 1976. "Ancestral Spirits and Hitchhiking Ghosts: Syncretism on Guam." *Midwestern Journal of Language and Folklore* 2:45–55.

Montell, William Lynwood. [1975] 1987. *Ghosts along the Cumberland: Deathlore in the Kentucky Foothills.* Reprint, Knoxville: University of Tennessee Press.

Moody, R. A. 1975. *Life after Life.* Covington, Georgia: Mockingbird Publishing.

Moorey, James. 1995. *Living with Grief and Mourning.* Manchester: Manchester University Press.

Mullen, Patrick B. 1978. *I Heard the Old Fisherman Say: Folklore of the Texas Gulf Coast.* Austin: University of Texas Press.

Musick, Ruth Ann. 1977. *Coffin Hollow and Other Ghost Tales.* Lexington: University of Kentucky Press.

Parkes, Colin Murray. 1964. "Effects of Bereavement on Physical and Mental Health: A Study of the Medical Records of Widows." *British Medical Journal* 2:271–79.

———. [1975] 1986. *Bereavement: Studies of Grief in Adult Life.* Reprint, Harmondsworth: Pelican.

"Alas, Poor Ghost!"

————. 1993. "Bereavement as a Psychosocial Transition: Processes of Adaptation to Change." In *Death, Dying, and Bereavement*, ed. Donna Dickenson and Malcolm Johnson. London, Newbury Park (California), and New Delhi: Sage Publications in association with the Open University. (Abridged from *Journal of Social Issues* 44 [1988]:53–65.)

Phillips, J. B. 1967. *Ring of Truth*. London: Hodder and Stoughton.

Polyani, Livia. 1979. "So What's the Point?" *Semiotica* 25:207–41.

Primiano, Leonard Norman. 1995. "Vernacular Religion and the Search for Method in Religious Folklife." *Western Folklore* 54:37–56.

Propp, Vladimir. 1968. *The Morphology of the Folktale*. 2d ed., revised and with a preface by Louis A. Wagner. Austin and London: University of Texas Press.

Prosterman, Annette. 1996. "Community and Societal Response to American Widows." In *Current Widowhood: Myths and Realities* by Helena Znaniecka Lopata. London and New Delhi: Sage.

Rees, W. Devi. 1974. "The Hallucinations of Widowhood." *British Medical Journal* 4:37–41.

"Reflexivity and the Study of Belief." 1995. Special issue of *Western Folklore* 54.

Ring, Kenneth. 1980. *Life at Death: A Scientific Investigation of the Near-Death Experience*. New York: Coward, McCann and Beoghegan.

Ring, Kenneth, and Stephen Franklin. 1981–82. "Do Suicide Survivors Report Near-Death Experiences?" *Omega* 12:191–208.

Roberts, Andy. 1987. "The Hitch Hiker from Space." *The Supernatural* 1:28–30.

Robinson, John. 1981. "Personal Narratives Reconsidered." *Journal of American Folklore* 94:58–85.

Rockwell, Joan. 1981. "The Ghosts of Evald Tang Kristensen." In *The Folklore of Ghosts*, ed. Hilda R. Ellis Davidson and W. M. S. Russell. Mistletoe Series. Bury St Edmunds: D. S. Brewer for the Folklore Society.

Roemer, Danielle. 1992. "The Personal Narrative and Salinger's *The Catcher in the Rye*." *Western Folklore* 51:5–10.

Rook, K. S. 1984. "The Negative Side of Social Interaction: Impact on Psychological Well-Being." *Journal of Personality and Social Psychology* 46:1097–1108.

————. 1989. "Strains in Older Adult's Friendships." In *Older Adult Friendship: Structure and Process*, ed. Grant G. Adams and R. Blieszner. Newbury Park, California: Sage.

Ross, Colin A., and Shaun Joshi. 1992. "Paranormal Experiences among the General Population." *Journal of Nervous and Mental Disease* 180:356–61.

Sacks, Harvey, Emmanuel Schegloff, and Gail Jefferson. 1978. "A Simplest Systematics for the Organization of Turn-Taking for Conversation." In *Studies in the Organization of Conversational Interaction*, ed. J. N. Schenkein. New York: Academic Press.

Sanders, Catherine M. 1989. *Grief: The Mourning After: Dealing with Adult Bereavement*. The Wiley Series on Personality Processes. New York, Chichester, Brisbane, Toronto, and Singapore: John Wiley and Sons.

Schulz, Richard. 1978. *The Psychology of Death, Dying, and Bereavement*. Reading, Pennsylvania: Addison-Wesley.

Shuchter, S. R., and S. Zisook. 1993. "The Course of Normal Grief." In *Handbook of Bereavement: Theory, Research, and Intervention*, ed. M. S. Stroebe, W. Stroebe, and R. O. Hansson. Cambridge: Cambridge University Press.

Sidgwick, (Mrs.), and Miss Alice Johnson. 1894. "Report of the Census of Hallucinations." *Proceedings of the Society for Psychical Research* 10.

Sidney, Sir Philip. [1598] 1959. "An Apology for Poetry." In *Sidney: An Apology for Poetry and Shelley: A Defence of Poetry*, ed. H. A. Needham. London: Ginn and Company.

Sinclair, George. [1685] 1969. *Satan's Invisible World Discovered*. Reprint, Gainsville, Florida: Scholar's Facsimiles and Reprints.

"Six Theories about Apparitions." 1956. *Proceedings of the Society for Psychical Research* 50.

Slotkin, Edgar. 1988. "Legend Genre as a Function of Audience." In *Monsters with Iron Teeth: Perspectives on Contemporary Legend*, vol. 3, ed. Gillian Bennett and Paul Smith. Sheffield: Sheffield Academic Press.

Spratt, Thomas. [1667] 1952. *The History of the Royal Society of London*, ed. J. I. Cape and H. W. Jones. Chicago: Encyclopedia Britannica.

Stahl, Sandra K. Dolby. 1977. "The Personal Narrative as Folklore." *Journal of the Folklore Institute* 14:19–30.

Stroebe, Margaret S., Robert O. Hansson, and Wolfgang Stroebe. 1993. "Contemporary Theories and Controversies in Bereavement Research." In *Handbook of Bereavement: Theory, Research, and Intervention*, ed. M. S. Stroebe, W. Stroebe, and R. O. Hansson. Cambridge: Cambridge University Press.

Stroebe, Margaret S., and Wolfgang Stroebe. 1993. "The Mortality of Bereavement: A Review." In *Handbook of Bereavement: Theory, Research, and Intervention*, ed. M. S. Stroebe, W. Stroebe, and R. O. Hansson. Cambridge: Cambridge University Press.

Sydow, Carl Wilhelm von. 1948. *Selected Papers on Folklore*. Copenhagen: Rosenkilde and Bagger.

Taillepied, Fr. Noel. [1588] n.d. *A Treatise of Ghosts*. Trans. and ed. Montague Summers. Reprint, London: Fortune Press.

Tedlock, Dennis. 1972. *Finding the Centre: Narrative Poetry of the Zuni Indians*. New York: Dial.

———. 1983. *The Spoken Word and the Work of Interpretation*. Philadelphia: University of Pennsylvania Press.

Thiselton Dyer, T. F. 1898. *The Ghost World*. London: Ward and Downey.

Thomas, Keith. 1971. *Religion and the Decline of Magic*. Letchworth: Weidenfeld and Nicolson.

Thomas, L. Eugene, Pamela E. Cooper, and David J. Suscovich. 1982–83. "Incidence of Near-Death and Intense Spiritual Experiences in an Intergenerational Sample: An Interpretation." *Omega* 13:35–41.

Toolan, Michael J. 1988. *Narrative: A Critical Linguistic Introduction*. London: Routledge.

Towler, Robert, et al. 1981–84. "Conventional Religion and Common Religion in Great Britain." In *Leeds Religious Research*. Leeds: University of Leeds, Department of Sociology.

Walker, Barbara, ed. 1995. *Out of the Ordinary: Folklore and the Supernatural*. Logan: Utah State University Press.

Walter, Tony. 1993. "Modern Death: Taboo or Not Taboo?" In *Death, Dying, and Bereavement*, ed. Donna Dickenson and Malcolm Johnson. London, Newbury Park (California), and New Delhi: Sage Publications in association with the Open University. (Abridged from *Sociology* 25 [1992]:293–310.)

Weiss, Robert S. 1982. "Attachment in Adults." In *The Place of Attachment in Human Behaviour*, ed. Colin Murray Parkes and Joan Stevenson-Hinde. New York: Basic Books.

———. 1993. "Loss and Recovery." In *Handbook of Bereavement: Theory, Research, and Intervention*, ed. M. S. Stroebe, W. Stroebe, and R. O. Hansson. Cambridge: Cambridge University Press.

Williams, Noel. 1983. *The Semantics of the Word 'Fairy' in English Between 1320 and 1829*. Ph.D. thesis, University of Sheffield.

Wilson, William A. 1975. "'The Vanishing Hitchhiker' among the Mormons." *Indiana Folklore* 8:79–97.

Wood, Charles Linley [Viscount Halifax]. 1936. *Lord Halifax's Ghost Book*. London: Geoffrey Bales.

Workman, Mark E. 1992. "Narratable and Unnarratable Lives." *Western Folklore* 51:97–107.

Index

forewarnings. *See under* psychic power

fortune-telling (*see also* spiritualism), 12, 17, 23–24, 26–27, 35, 51, 67–69, 72

Freud, Sigmund, 81–82, 113

G
ghosts. *See* hauntings
Goldsmith, Oliver, 146–47
Gorer, Geoffrey, 10, 15, 100

H
Hand, Wayland D., 2
hauntings, 2, 5, 11–13, 17, 22, 24, 41–51, 67, 115, 145–50, 162–65
heaven and hell. *See* afterlife
history of belief. *See* supernatural: history of belief in
horoscopes. *See* fortune-telling
houses, things in. *See* hauntings
Hufford, David, 3, 32

I
immortality. *See* afterlife
intuition, 24, 62–63, 67, 72

J
Jones, Louis C., 11

K
Kübler-Ross, Elisabeth, 82

L
lady in white. *See under* motifs
Lang, Andrew, 2, 32, 145, 150–59
language. *See* phraseology
Larkin, Philip, 113–14

Lavater, Lewes (Ludowig), 141, 159

Leeds University, 10, 12

legends (*see also* folk belief; motifs), 3–5, 9, 39, 41, 124, 159–68

the Leicester study, 79–80, 83, 91, 109, 115, 178–82

Lewis, C. S., 100–101

life after death. *See* afterlife

Lindemann, Erich, 81–82, 98, 113

linguistics. *See* phraseology

literature. *See* media

M
the Manchester study, 3, 12, 18, 115, 173–77

materialist. *See* rationalist world view

mediums. *See* fortune-telling; spiritualism

memorates: described, 3–5, 39, 174, 183–88; analyzed, 51–52, 56–58, 115–37

Montell, William Lynwood, 2, 11

morality. *See under* tradition and belief

motifs, 14, 22, 41–45, 48–50, 58, 66, 142, 153; white ladies, 5, 59, 170

N
nightmares. *See* dreams

O
omens. *See* motifs; psychic power: forewarnings

P
Palladino, Eusapia, 156
Parkes, Colin Murray, 88, 90, 99

"Alas, Poor Ghost!"

Phillips, J. B., 100–101
phraseology, 14–17, 41, 75, 80,
    109–11, 168–70, 176–77
poltergeists. See hauntings
precognition. See psychic power:
    clairvoyance
premonitions. See psychic
    power: forewarnings
presence, sense of (see also dead,
    contact with), 11–12,
    15–16, 24, 40–43, 45–46,
    49–50, 59–60, 66, 77–80,
    91, 98–113
psychic power, 26, 55, 67,
    152–54; clairvoyance,
    11–12, 28; forewarnings, 2,
    14, 17, 21, 24, 35, 58, 67,
    132–33; telepathy, 11–12,
    14, 17, 20, 24, 54, 59, 66

R
rationalist world view, 2, 11,
    14–15, 25–28, 31–36, 38,
    109–10, 112, 145–46,
    150–59
religion and belief, 12–13,
    25–27, 35–36, 39, 64, 66,
    73, 139–43, 152, 164, 172

S
Sanders, Catherine, 82–83, 94
science. See rationalist world
    view
seances. See under spiritualism
Shakespeare, 1, 139–45
society. See family; tradition and
    belief
Society for Psychical Research
    (SPR), 151–54, 171
spirits. See dead, contact with;
    presence, sense of

spiritualism (see also fortune-
    telling), 70–72, 91, 97,
    103–4, 110; seances, 34,
    67, 73–75, 141, 153–54
Stahl, Sandra, 4
stereotypes (see also motifs), 1,
    39, 41, 46, 141, 166–67
stories. See memorates
supernatural: history of belief in,
    2, 9, 30–33, 36, 44,
    139–43, 145–46, 161–62,
    164–65, 168–72; in media,
    1, 5, 9–10, 39, 49, 109,
    139, 146, 168
supernaturalist world view, 15,
    17, 25–29, 31–32, 36–38,
    49, 110–12, 150–59

T
taboo. See evil; fortune-telling;
    spiritualism
telepathy. See under psychic
    power
Thomas, Keith, 29, 139
tradition and belief (see also
    rationalist world view;
    supernaturalist world
    view), 5, 31, 35–39, 45,
    66–67, 140–42, 168–69;
    morality, 12, 18, 24–25, 75

V
Vázsonyi, Andrew, 124, 129
visitations. See dead, contact with

W
warnings. See psychic power:
    forewarnings
white ladies. See under motifs
witnesses. See family
wraiths, 2, 56–57, 64, 164